A GARDEN
FOR ALL
SEASONS

A GARDEN FOR ALL SEASONS

Chicago Botanic Garden

Chicago Horticultural Society

Founded 1890

Photographs by Arthur Lazar

Text by Jay Pridmore

Design by William A. Seabright

Archivist William Aldrich

A *Garden for All Seasons* was produced for the Chicago Horticultural Society
by William A. Seabright Graphic Design

Text and Design Copyright © 1990 the Chicago Horticultural Society

Photographs Copyright © 1990 Arthur Lazar

All the photographs for *A Garden for All Seasons*
were taken at the Chicago Botanic Garden
from January 1988 to December 1989.

First published in the United States
of America in 1990 by the
Chicago Horticultural Society
P.O. Box 400
Glencoe, Illinois 60022-0400

ISBN: 0-939914-06-9

Dedication

Harold Byron Smith has served as a member of the Board of Directors of the Chicago Horticultural Society for twenty-four years.

Mr. Smith's varied contributions to the Society and the Botanic Garden began even before he became a director. In 1964, as a member of the Cook County Forest Preserve Advisory Committee, he was one of a small group of visionary leaders who formulated the plan establishing the Garden on its present site and providing that it be managed by the Horticultural Society. The most recent example of his longstanding commitment and generosity is his decision to underwrite the publication of this book in connection with the Society's centennial celebration and the Garden's twenty-fifth year.

Mr. Smith's love of people has inevitably drawn his attention to the human as well as the scientific side of the Garden. He has been ever mindful of the Garden's role as a place for people to enjoy as well as learn, and has taken a keen interest in the needs of visitors. As an individual he has enjoyed a mutually affectionate friendship with the staff and his fellow directors.

As the Botanic Garden builds an even greater following in future years, and as it influences the Chicago area in many positive ways, it owes a significant debt to Harold Byron Smith. His vision and kindness have left a lasting mark on the Garden, its people, and the community that benefits by its presence.

Contents

Introduction

The Centennial Celebration of the Chicago Horticultural Society is a time to reflect on the important contributions that the Society has made to the quality of life in Chicago.

It has been twenty-five years since an inspired collaboration between the Cook County Forest Preserve District and the Horticultural Society, led by William A.P. Pullman, created the Botanic Garden. Since then, the foresight of past Board Chairmen Peter H. Merlin, Ralph A. Bard, Jr. and Nancy Race, along with a determined staff and membership, have built an institution of strength and diversity.

Maintaining the Botanic Garden as a place of inspirational beauty remains preeminent among our goals. Visitors who return year after year will see increasingly lush grounds, unique new gardens, and an ever-larger variety of plants.

Closely connected to our aesthetic role is education. The Society's mission "to stimulate and develop an interest in, an appreciation for, and an understanding of gardening..." has led to classroom and outreach programs in topics ranging from prairie restoration to urban gardening.

Moreover, programs in research are presently building a stronger foundation for the Garden. Horticulturists are involved in various projects to evaluate plants for our area, and save others that might be threatened. Efforts such as these help us to expand our palette of plants, not only in the Botanic Garden, but throughout the region as well.

Building a many-dimensioned "living museum" has required the dedicated efforts of many: our Board of Directors, the Woman's Board, devoted volunteers, generous benefactors, and a highly skilled staff led by Director Roy L. Taylor.

The Garden's work is now more important than ever. In a world that cries for conservation, the Society's overriding purpose is to demonstrate the precious value of the Earth's garden, and to influence the public to join our efforts to cultivate and preserve it.

Janet Meakin Poor
Chairman of the Board

Spring

At its soul, and especially in spring, the Chicago Botanic Garden is a place of splendid contradictions. The Garden reflects the delicate relationship between man and nature, which is often overlooked and neglected. But here we witness a place nurtured by human hand, by years of acquired knowledge and labor. The effect is one of unshattered, quiet balance.

The unknowable, almost mystical quality of the Garden is not far from its surface. The landscape exhibits shapes and colors as exacting as those in a woodblock print. Yet its character, its very composition, changes constantly. Time and nature conspire here, with results that are at once astonishing and serene.

Gardens inspire artists of all kinds, but they never exhaust the muse, and only rarely capture it. Painters recreate gentle lines of landscape and sometimes produce striking vibrations of color, but their pictures are only metaphors for phenomena far larger than the canvas. Poets describe the mysterious intentions of nature. Here too, words evoke only moments in the broad sweep of the seasons. The Garden resists comprehension. Still, we are enriched by attempts to understand it more deeply, more clearly.

Is the Garden elusive and obscure? Perhaps. But it is also luxurious and generous. It caresses all the senses, and does so in ways that are never quite predictable. Early flowers force themselves through barely thawed soil, reveling in warmer air, and then withstanding a late drop of snow. New color in flowering trees invites us out onto grounds that were inhospitable only weeks before. Spring flora inspires many reactions, from irrepressibility, to optimism, to romance.

The delicate powers of nature have fascinated mankind all through history, and for centuries gardening has counted among civilization's most important pastimes. No other art is so consistently heightened by invisible forces. Horticulturists live in a world defined by the boundless laws of evolution and propagation. They attempt to codify nature's miracles, if only to influence the outcome slightly. It is a worthwhile and most patient discipline.

Chicagoans have long understood the impact of gardens. In 1837, the city adopted the motto *Urbs in Horto* ("city in a garden") for its corporate seal. In 1853, a local journal called *Prairie Farmer* urged the formation of a 300-acre garden on the outskirts of the city. In 1890, when a true botanic garden was still a distant prophecy, a number of local devotees chartered the Chicago Horticultural Society. Its first task, hardly modest, was to organize horticultural exhibitions for the 1893 World's Columbian Exposition.

Make no little plans. They have no magic...Let your watchword be "order" and your beacon "beauty."

Daniel Burnham, architect and Director of Public Works for the World's Columbian Exposition, 1893

The city fathers were enchanted by the natural landscape of their shoreline and prairies. They were also determined, by force of will, to create a city of gardens as well as industry. For the Exposition, the Society was given an active role, helping to organize scores of acres of waterways and naturalistic plantings, some of which remain on Chicago's South Side. The plants included native grasses, willow trees, bulbous flowering plants, and seventy-five carloads of herbaceous aquatics brought from surrounding states. The design was conceived by Frederick Law Olmstead, and visitors from all over the world came to witness brocades of green space woven through the White City palaces. More significantly, the fair set a tone for parks and planting that has endured throughout Chicago and the area surrounding the city.

It is uncommon for a garden to have such a water feature as this. When visitors cross onto the main island, they surely feel that they have left the everyday world… We wanted to keep cars away as much as possible, and that visitors should walk to the Education Center. This is very import-ant when you are working so closely with nature.

Edward Larrabee Barnes,
architect for the Education
Center, built in 1976

The Society was sustained through the efforts of powerful philanthropists such as Charles Hutchinson. He was a banker, president of the Chicago Board of Trade, and a founder of the Art Institute. Between 1910 and 1912, he was president of the Horticultural Society. Among his many gifts to the city was a medal that he commissioned during a visit to Sweden. Today, the Hutchinson Medal is awarded annually by the Society to individuals who have made substantial contributions to the practice of horticulture. Civic leaders, scientists and herbalists have been among those honored. The medal symbolizes one of Hutchinson's lasting contributions—a vision that the quality of life in Chicago would be enhanced by sedulous attention to gardens.

In its early days, Society members were leaders in the adoption of Daniel Burnham's Plan of Chicago, proposed in 1909. That plan would preserve the lakefront and inland beltways to create one of the world's most beautiful garden cities. The Society also supported the efforts of the Chicago Park District to develop an expansive system of conservatories. In the 1940s, it opened a Garden Center at the Chicago Public Library as a resource for private gardeners to beautify their homes. These efforts illustrate that even before opening a garden of its own, the Horticultural Society exerted vital influence on our physical environment.

Early in the 1960s, the Society engaged itself in a new role, as the builder and keeper of a botanic garden. Various sites were contemplated, a space in Chicago's Grant Park among them. Then in 1963, under the leadership of Chicago business leader William A.P. Pullman, himself a dedicated gardener, the Society was offered Forest Preserve land on the northern edge of Cook County. After negotiations, the Cook County Forest Preserve District joined with the Chicago Horticultural Society to develop a 300-acre garden along Edens Expressway. Parcels that included a lowland marsh, once on the edge of several North Shore farms, would undergo a remarkable transformation.

The layout of the garden was the work of landscape architect John O. Simonds of Pittsburgh, who envisioned hillocks and waterways reminiscent of the Garden of Perfect Brightness, built near Beijing in 1709. Elevated landforms served the purpose of providing protection from harsh winds. Water offered a measure of peacefulness and light, and also the practical benefit of a home for many aquatic plants. In those early years, and with the vision of Simonds' young associate Geoffrey L. Rausch, the Garden was endowed with a blueprint of nine islands amidst sixty acres of water. It would be improved and refined in the years to come.

My first look at the site for the Botanic Garden came on a cold, windy day in April. The first mound along the Edens Expressway was in place and a large sign indicating that a botanic garden was under construction was ready for background planting. The wind and sticky, impermeable clay were warnings that we were facing a long and difficult task, and that patience would be our greatest virtue.

Dr. Francis de Vos, first director of the Botanic Garden, in his farewell remarks in 1976.

For most visitors, their first glimpse of the Botanic Garden is not a garden at all, but Turnbull Woods. This area was noted for its natural flora as early as 1917, when the Forest Preserve District began acquiring land from a local landowner, William James Davis Turnbull, who used the area for light grazing and little else. Today, parts of this area have evolved into woodland, where spring ephemerals command attention while the air is still heavy with early season thaw. Their colors come initially in subtle clusters, later in profusion.

Among flowers in the woods, bloodroot (*Sanguinaria canadensis*) is plentiful, but also elusive because its flower is fragile and can be broken apart easily by wind or rain. The eight-petaled flower enlivens the forest floor with intense whites and porcelain-like form. While bloodroot provides a moment of brightness, it also connects us to the history of our area. Indians and pioneers used its toxic juices for health-giving properties derived when swallowed in small doses.

The early spring woods is a time of curious forms, such as the cut-leaved toothwort (*Dentaria laciniata*) with clusters of small, white, crown-like flowers over sharp-toothed leaves. The white trout lily (*Erythronium albidum*) has a leafless stem and flower that explodes with long, narrow petals and sepals.

As the season warms, the ground in Turnbull Woods fills in more thickly with color. White trillium (*Trillium grandiflorum*) creates carpets that can change from perfect white to faint pink in the weeks that it flowers in May. Quieter are the primeval-looking Dutchman's breeches (*Dicentra cucullaria*). On these long stems, as many as ten small flowers, each shaped like a butterfly or a pair of breeches, hang lightly over greenish-blue fern-like leaves.

Another portion of Turnbull Woods is a place with different charms, and also of intense interest to scientists. It is an authentic and intact prairie savanna, where native oaks and other scattered trees are spaced sufficiently to allow the sun to support many sedges and wildflowers that are native to this habitat. Before settlement, savannas represented a delicate balance of nature that rarely exists on its own. On the edge of the vast Midwest prairie, savannas were subject to fires that would roar across the land from the west. Fire was important as it cleared shrubs and saplings that could in time create a forest. Only the most durable trees survived, along with specially adapted plants. Today, vestiges of this community remain, thanks in part to Mr. Turnbull's grazing cattle. Savanna plants are represented by Pennsylvania sedge (*Carex pennsylvanica*), golden alexander (*Zizea aurea*), and bluestem goldenrod

In rugged natural beauty and splendid growth of timber no woodland acquired by the Board equals the Turnbull tract which lies along the north county line and Green Bay Road, a short distance above Glencoe…The tract was obtained from the United States in 1843 by Alexander Brand, one of Chicago's first bankers. By him, it was transferred to Thomas Turnbull in 1852. The same year Thomas Turnbull gave the land to his son, William James Davis Turnbull, who sold it to the Forest Preserve District. The fine old homestead in which Mr. Turnbull still lives is one of the landmarks of the early settlement of the north shore.

Peter Reinberg, President of the Cook County Forest Preserve District, shortly after the 1917 purchase of a portion of Turnbull Woods.

(*Solidago caesia*). They are deeply rooted enough to survive an early spring fire, and they wane when a lack of fire creates thicker canopies and more shade.

To save these species, garden naturalists have recently begun a program of controlled burns in the area, conducted in random years to replicate the sporadic nature of prairie fires. In time, hopes are for a richer-looking savanna. Sedges and wildflowers will grow abundantly, die off, and create flammable hay as the remains are dried by springtime breezes. Fires will complete the cycle—releasing nutrients in the soil and clearing weeds and woody plants that would otherwise alter this valuable tract of land.

Success of this kind fulfills an important mission of the Botanic Garden—that of a "Noah's Ark" for plants. This is vital work because of natural habitat being destroyed and plant species being threatened throughout our region. To battle against such calamities, members of the Garden staff have traveled to Indiana, for example, to collect seed of a small tree called American snowbell (*Styrax americana*), which was once reported to be extinct. Horticulturists have also searched for willow oak (*Quercus phellos*) in the Cache River Basin in southern Illinois. The potential of projects such as these is to preserve genetically pure strains of species for collections and research.

You really had to be a dreamer to imagine what the Botanic Garden would ultimately become. But nature, in its wisdom, has a way of softening the land-scape, making it blend so gracefully...The Garden is now one of the great cultural assets of the Chicago metro-politan area, and its impor-tance increases every day. It makes our whole area a better place in which to live.

Arthur L. Janura, General Superintendent, Cook County Forest Preserve District

As the warmth of the season advances, effortless, endless new life overtakes the Garden. In French countrysides, spring was the time preferred by Impressionist artists, when the varied tints of fresh grass and flowering trees contributed to visual symphonies. For such painters, it was the season for wide, contoured views, of distant fields defined by vibrating patterns of color. For us too, it is a time of amazing activity, of movement and sublime balance.

The extroverts of the season, of course, are the flowering trees and shrubs. Diverse magnolias (*Magnolia* spp.) are plentiful throughout the Garden, with intense profusions of white, sometimes with pink tints, serving as attractive landmarks amidst stoic, anonymous pines. Several types of magnolia present here came from China in the 1700s, where they grew beside the doors of temples. For us, their flowers risk harm from a late frost, but barring such mishap, they provide immensely colorful and fragrant rewards.

Another early performance in spring is that of eastern redbud (*Cercis canadensis*), an ethereal tree with vibrant pink flowers coming at a time when other plants appear unmoved by the slightly warmer air. By May, flowering begins in earnest. Selkirk crabapples (*Malus* 'Selkirk') show mauve flowers, stunning next to the broadening green backdrops of the season. Various hawthorns (*Crataegus* spp.) are clustered close to paths and roadways; they flower, seemingly all at once, and make effortless our first long walks on the grounds. Pussy willows (*Salix discolor*) are another pleasure of the season. Their bright yellow anthers glisten in the early May sun, and provide handsome curtains beside yellow tulips and nearby drifts of narcissus, now coming up by the hundreds.

While the luminescence of flowering trees caresses the eyes, other sensations also make their way directly into the spirit. Canada geese are now year-round residents of the Garden, but they are particularly animated in spring. Flocks inspect lawns beside lakes, and new goslings swim easily along the shore.

Fragrance can be sparing in early spring, but by May, distinct scents of flowering shrubs cling to the fresh breeze, and they draw visitors down meandering paths, such as those in the Edna Kanaley Graham Bulb Garden. The citrus-like smell of the mockorange (*Philadelphus* 'Silver Showers'), for example, provides a fast memory for this place at this time. The Koreanspice viburnum (*Viburnum carlesii*), growing against the Bulb Garden's limestone wall, provides a sharper fragrance, another invisible but unmistakable imprint of the season.

The Japanese Garden has been a
spectacular success. It is one of the few
gardens we have that is as interesting
in winter as it is in summer. This is a
unique garden, something the average
person does not often see. It is a new
experience for most people. I love to go
there and simply walk around.
It is very beautiful.

Ralph A. Bard, Jr., Chairman of the
Board of Directors, 1979-1986

Activity in the Bulb Garden comes in a succession of phases, first discrete, later overlapping. The early phases are defined by a few flowers that challenge the final stages of winter. Snowdrops (*Galanthus nivalis*), for example, come up in clusters in early April, before any but the most anxious bulb lovers have ventured out to witness their stirrings. Then come crocuses (*Crocus chrysanthus*), strong perennials that open and close their fine flowers in response to the momentary intensity of the sun. Short-stemmed crocus cultivars—'Blue Pearl' and 'Cream Beauty' for example—look natural, if isolated, under still dormant trees. A little later, hybrids such as 'Remembrance' and white-flowered 'Peter Pan' come up taller and, as hybrids commonly are, showier.

Also in April, waterlily tulips (*Tulipa kaufmanniana*) rise quickly to their height of eight to ten inches and flex slightly in the brisk spring air. Other early sirens of spring include the guinea-hen flower (*Fritillaria meleagris*), with deep hues and conspicuous checkering on its petals. "One square is of greenish yellow, and the other purple, keeping the same order on the backside of the flower as on the inside," wrote Dodonaeus, the 16th-Century Flemish botanist. "Every leaf seemeth to be the feather of a Ginnie hen."

Wild tulips predominate in the Bulb Garden, chosen because they perform most reliably as perennials. Unlike rich carpets of solid color, such wild species are noted for curious individual characteristics. The lady tulip (*Tulipa clusiana*) has alternating white petals inside and bright red petals out. When closed, the flower appears cherry red, and in the warmth it opens flat, almost entirely white. In between, which is usual, vertical stripes identify this tulip unambiguously.

Wild tulips (*Tulipa tarda* and *T. acuminata*) provide more intimate pleasures than extravagant ones. But at least once in spring they make an indelible impression—such as when new bulbs come up and flower in the same instant that a nearby crabapple tree blossoms in precisely the same hue. Such moments, of course, cannot be predicted with certainty, nor should they.

Many other compositions, planned in fall and imagined all winter, are now being realized. Narcissus (*Narcissus* spp.), happily, are ubiquitous —found wherever a small patch of ground can support a friendly streak of spring color. Many varieties have been cultivated over the years, and dozens are used throughout the grounds. In the Bulb Garden, masses of 'Mt. Hood' create a white foreground, over which hang crown imperials (*Fritillaria imperialis*) with an orange that appears to glow in the presence of these subdued companions.

As the season moves along, a great variety of other perennials in the demonstration gardens arouse intense interest. Peonies (*Paeonia* spp.) show endless variations of color—the yellow spectrum includes greenish yellow, buttery yellow and other still paler hues. A few are strongly colored, such as the orange-reds and magentas. A number of the Japanese peonies have flowers with contrasting colors: red with yellow centers, pink and red, white and gold. Sometimes colored petals have edges of a slightly different shade. Such variations can be closely noted, of course, because the dimensions of the bush and the fragrance of the flower invite close inspection. Connoisseurs, quickly made, will argue happily for their preferences.

Irises are also common in spring, coming early in the form of netted iris (*Iris reticulata*) with its varying shades of blue and violet. These flowers are smaller than the later-blooming kinds, but have been known to poke through barely thawed soil and even brave a late snowfall, along with snowdrops and crocuses.

Later on, irises come in their familiar way, seductive and plentiful. Bearded iris is the common name for rhizomes that flower in seemingly endless colors, from a pale straw to dark rose-violet. All are proud and even extravagant—their configuration of upright and descending petals gives each flower a certain sculptural quality. From time to time, the colorful variety of irises will produce a clash. But this is a matter of taste, a luxury afforded by the hardiness and long season of the genus. And for that they win our affection. They come early in spring and stay late. They attach themselves to delicate, invigorating, romantic and colorful memories of a time of year that is all of these things.

It has been suggested that the challenge of late spring is to not love it too much. Some of the Garden's grandest compositions take place in April and May, with wood hyacinth and camassia flowering tall and elegant behind naturalized bulb flowers which are never more abundant. It is also a time for primroses, pansies and poppies, each of them striking. Taken together they set the garden ablaze. What can possibly be left for summer?

Other sections of the Botanic Garden are also crowded with their own springtime theatrics. Among the most interesting are those of the Rock Garden, where whitlow grass (*Draba aizoides*) and pasque flower (*Anemone pulsatilla*) illustrate typical adaptations for rugged mountain environments. Strong roots, low-growing flowers, rich color, and a preference for well-drained soil are among the characteristics shared by these plants.

So, too, do the ericaceous plants flourish. Not native to our area, azaleas, rhododendrons, and other colorful spring bushes are happiest when specially provided with acid soil and protection from wind and unremitting sun. These plants come originally from gentler climates than ours, so horticulturists place them near walls and under large pines to provide protection from wind and sun. To the surprise of many, they grow and flower splendidly in spring, especially the hybrid *Rhododendron* 'P.J.M.' a welcomed development which truly overcomes the severe weather of Chicago.

Everywhere in spring, the Garden provides activity that we do not quite expect. Inspired relationships of color and form—a woods, a waterfall, a Japanese promenade—are especially open and inviting in spring. They massage the senses. They touch the spirit. They encourage the visitor to look deeper at the landscape, draw closer to the flora. Their messages are never more optimistic than they are right now. Quiet and peaceful business abounds. The Garden in spring provides moments of perfection.

The main reason we do not see more poppies, even in sunny cottage-type gardens, is simply that we think of them in the spring, which is too late to plant either seeds or roots. Let us think of them in June, the correct time, and prepare a small bed— or a large one—that can be very lightly scratched in August, and the seeds sown.

Henry Mitchell, author, from The Essential Earthman, *1981*

Summer

Summer arrives before we beckon it. It is the long season, of mixed impressions, when the extroverted atmosphere of spring is replaced with something lush and mature. The summer might begin amidst careless optimism. But ultimately, it is a time of concentration. In hot Midwest sun, the green backdrops deepen. Foliage weighs heavily on branches. Durability is valued. The fragile recede.

Yet the Botanic Garden continues to exhibit wonderful patterns. Summer differs from spring in that it engages the mind more than it caresses the senses. But even if summer's messages are less exuberant, it transmits far-reaching lessons about mankind's relationship to the natural world. In this sense, the Gertrude B. Nielsen Heritage Garden is an appropriate introduction to the rest of the Garden. Besides being a verdant and relaxing place, it explains much about the basic science and natural history of plants.

The Heritage Garden forms a circle, two quadrants of which are devoted to the concept of taxonomy, focusing on resemblances within plant families and contrasts among them. Ferns (Pteridophyta) are primitive plants which reproduce from spores. Grasses (Poaceae) produce stamens that hang loosely in the air. Iris (Iridaceae) unfurls a distinctive, colorful three-petaled flower. Among many other plant families, sunflowers (Asteraceae) have protected seeds, enabling them to survive so effortlessly on roadsides and in vacant lots.

Geographic beds, also in the Heritage Garden, exhibit the diversity of plant life from continent to continent. In this area we learn that eastern North America is home to smooth hydrangea (*Hydrangea arborescens*) and that prairie gentian (*Eustoma grandiflorum*) comes originally from the American Southwest and Mexico. Another label tells the story of naturalists who made an early expedition to South America in 1799, and returned to Europe with 6,200 new species. "The earth is overloaded with plants," wrote one of these explorers, Alexander von Humboldt, in his South American journals. "Nothing impedes their free growth."

The design for the Heritage Garden was modeled after the oldest botanic garden in Europe, that in Padua, Italy. Built in 1545, the Padua garden marks an important point in the history of horticulture. It was there that naturalists defined botany as a science and simultaneously treated cultivation as an art. From that point on, the plant world would draw increasing attention from scholars, architects, aristocrats and others who would eventually develop the field of horticulture.

To commemorate this marriage of scholarship and romance, Mrs. Nielsen also funded the commissioning of the Carolus Linnaeus sculpture, by Robert Berks. Linnaeus, a Swedish botanist born in 1707, is considered the father of modern taxonomy. He developed binomial nomenclature, which identifies all plants by genus and species. The adoption of Linnaeus' system advanced the cause of botany, and ultimately inspired gardens such as this one—scientific places of the most exquisite earthly delights.

If the summer garden stimulates the mind, the Japanese Garden, Sansho-En, reaches past the intellect and toward the soul. Gardens like this one—of symbolic and idealized form—were first built in Japan over a millennium ago, to provide war lords with respite from their historic turmoil. They were places to contemplate the noble aims of Buddha, focusing primarily on the belief that all suffering is caused by want, and its cure is to eliminate craving.

Each Japanese garden follows a unique design, but most derive from a common theme. With the adoption of monastic Zen philosophy in Japan in the 1300s, gardens typically were built to inspire meditation and to achieve "absolute emptiness." Enlightenment and bliss of such magnitude resist description, but one obvious requirement is oneness with nature. Thus monks also became gardeners, with the responsibility to promote naturalness, elegance and subtlety in the physical environment. Gardens need not be large, but they should express serenity and permanence.

Sansho-En means "garden of three islands," which describes a man-made creation, but also a symbolic version of the world as we might imagine it. From a distance, the islands have the mystical quality of "floating worlds." Perspective plays tricks: The scene lies composed in a broad panorama. Yet the gardens remain close and reveal intimate details across the water. The islands are dotted with large field stones, symbols of the earth's bones or skeleton underneath. But the striking horizontality of its composition makes the garden appear only lightly anchored, somehow movable.

The cypress wood bridge that connects the outside world to Keiunto, "the island of the auspicious cloud," is arched, a device that encourages visitors, quite unconsciously, to pause at its apex. Here we witness typical asymmetry, which the Japanese find more evocative than the artifice of perfect balance. At the end of the bridge and to one side is a large willow (*Salix alba* var. *tristis*), uncannily resembling a curtain held back to reveal the gentle dramas inside. Beyond this point, the garden shows dense growth of green foliage. We walk forward effortlessly. Paths are partly hidden, but the direction is always suggested.

In spring and early summer, rhododendrons and azaleas provide seasonal interest in this garden. But the Japanese understand that color is essentially ephemeral, and the trappings of mature form are more highly valued. A Peking cotoneaster (*Cotoneaster acutifolius*), Nanking cherry (*Prunus tomentosa*) and star magnolia (*Magnolia stellata*) appear randomly placed, but they are pruned uniformly so that their branches draw close to the ground. They appear old and venerable, not cultivated by human device, but wrought, instead, by the long, patient forces of the earth.

Conifers, especially Scots pine (*Pinus sylvestris*), are the dominant tree throughout Sansho-En. Like many species here, this one is not native to

Japan. But as a symbol in the garden, its meaning is unmistakable. The whisperings of wind through conifers' needles express the wish for a long and happy life. Their evergreen hue is a constant reminder of the everlastingness of nature. The exotic archings of the trunks and branches, trained with wires to affect great age, amplify the simple but profound respect for longevity that is expressed constantly in Japanese culture.

Sansho-En was completed in 1982 by Koichi Kawana, a Los Angeles landscape architect heavily imbued in traditional Japanese values. "Visual entities which appear as design in the Western sense," Kawana has written, "are less important than the invisible philosophical, religious and symbolic elements." Curiously, perhaps typically, Kawana began this project with only a generalized plan for the islands. As he became more familiar with the site and the species appropriate for the climate, he made planting decisions, and the outcome is filled with natural harmonies that belie the hand of man. Isolated field stones and shrubs are joined in subtle compositions. Paths disappear in foliage or over land forms. Small stone steps present a sudden, new possibility. These vignettes are executed with such skill that they draw out a constant flow of pleasant, contemplative thoughts.

Sansho-En merits an extended visit, which is appropriate given the Japanese belief that things mature with time. In the dry gardens, we see an expanse of fine gravel raked in waves to symbolize water. Such features are meant to suggest that the essence of the sea, its isolation, can be captured as poignantly on land as on the water itself. Near the dry garden, a subtle contrast lies in the moss garden—lush, fragile and accessible only over the stone steps that bisect it. And beyond those steps, a shelter of translucent panels, the *shoin*, transports the visitor still further into the reflective world. Near the door, a water basin serves the ritual of symbolic purification before entering. Inside, the *shoin* is simple, nearly monastic, but its proportions, and the harmonious parallel lines of its architecture, label the building with obvious nobility.

As the visitor encounters the zig-zag bridge, leading to Seifuto, or the "island of clear, pure breezes," one finds cattails, iris and willow mingling in a still channel, separate but connected to the open waters of the symbolic sea that surrounds most of Sansho-En. The bridge itself is peculiar but symbolically useful. It provides an escape from evil spirits, who are quick of foot but travel only in straight lines. Mortals who are pursued by them can easily negotiate the crooked turn in this bridge; the unwanted specter most certainly will plunge headlong into the water.

Simplicity must not be confused with plainness which is, in many cases monotonous or a lack of refinement. Simplicity means the achievement of maximum effect with minimum means.

Koichi Kawana, landscape architect and designer of Sansho-En

Across another strait is Horaijima, the "garden of everlasting happiness." No access is provided to Horaijima as tradition reserves this island for immortals. But the view is paradisaical. Its lines mimic a much longer and more distant mountain range, an effect reinforced by Horaijima's sparser plantings. This image is never stronger than on mornings when thick mist rises up from the water.

Creating a microcosm of another kind is the objective of the Ellen Thorne Smith Naturalistic Garden, in winding paths on the edge of the Home Landscape Demonstration Gardens. The focus of this garden is on the wild plants of the Illinois woodland and prairie, natives that are increasingly rare. It is a place for wildflowers and grasses often used in modern horticulture, and which connect today's gardens with flora that evolved here over many centuries.

Seasonal changes in the Naturalistic Garden reflect the many changes that occur in woodland and on prairie over the course of a season. In June, spring ephemerals among the oaks and hickories have receded, but many plants remain active and colorful, some with berries and fruit. Red baneberry (*Actaea rubra*) gives a white flower in spring, clusters of glistening scarlet berries in early summer, and it retains a fern-like leaf for several months thereafter. Early summer is also time for highbush blueberry (*Vaccinium corymbosum*). This shrub, abundant with fruit throughout much of June, provides the added interest of attracting birds, some as colorful as orioles and cardinals.

Beyond the small woodland, a separate section of the Naturalistic Garden is planted with species typical of the Illinois prairie. Here, too, color and texture change gradually as the season moves along. By early summer, many striking wildflowers have died. But overall colors ripen. Asters and goldenrod grow amidst the native grasses, such as finely-textured June grass (*Koeleria cristata*). The canvas fills in nicely, and in evening light, blue and yellow flowers, along with the varied greens of grass and foliage, lay themselves out in a soft and most graceful palette. It seems, at least for a moment, that the ideal Midwestern garden is one as unhewn as this.

People who are visually impaired, we find, approach life with a sensitivity that might elude those who take sight, sound and mobility for granted. With this in mind, the Sensory Garden was developed as a place for plants to stimulate the full range of perception—not just sight but smell, sound and touch as well.

Funded by the William T. Bacon, Sr. family in 1987, the Sensory Garden is on a peninsula, often surrounded by geese, honking like klaxons and flapping like luffing sails. In many ways, signals like these give the visitor a sense of topography and environment. Near the entrance, a thick clump of Ravenna grass (*Erianthus ravennae*) sounds a hard rustle in the slightest wind. Further along on the garden path, the copper roof of a small shelter vibrates with persistent tapping when it rains.

Not all persons who are visually impaired live in utter darkness, and for them the raised beds along the eastern walk, the morning side walk, of the Sensory Garden hold striking shapes and colors. Garden peonies (*Paeonia* hybrids) can be as large as grapefruits. Others, such as sweet false chamomile (*Matricaria recutita*) and white-leaf everlasting (*Helichrysum angustifolium*), feature both distinctive forms and fragrances. And for touching, Rober's lemon rose geranium (*Pelargonium graveolens* 'Rober's Lemon Rose') is large, statuesque and soft.

The garden is generous. A hand run across the thick, furry rug of wooly thyme (*Thymus pseudolanuginosus*) comes up with a scent that is fresh, sweet and intoxicating in its intensity. While many shrubs are hard and abrasive, branches of delicate tamarisk (*Tamarix ramosissima* 'Summer Glow') hang lightly out over the path. As we brush against them with bare arms, they feel as soft and refined as they look.

We can walk to a shore, over which a deck is built, and visitors can enjoy southern sun and breeze across the lake. Well within arm's length are lotus plants (*Nelumbo* spp.), with their huge, glaucous, waxy leaves. Another trail leads to the woodland meadow, a setting favored by Mrs. Bacon. Here the tenacious wind, especially in afternoon, rakes the sparse leaves of young birch trees (*Betula populifolia* and *B. platyphylla japonica* 'Whitespire'). These sounds, along with the escape of ground squirrels and the fuller rustle of sugar maples (*Acer saccharum*), become more articulate with each passing moment. Further along, the direct warmth of the sun suggests a treeless meadow. Some visitors take this opportunity to sit in the grass and enjoy the calm. Experiences of this sort, like the entire Sensory Garden, were designed specifically for persons who are visually impaired, but it enables all the Garden's visitors to reaffirm a relationship with nature that is personal and ineffable, but also universal.

A broad streak of Midwest informality characterizes one of the Botanic Garden's favorite attractions. The Bruce Krasberg Rose Garden varies distinctly from the predominantly rectangular rosariums that are found in most other large gardens. Built in 1985, the Rose Garden eschews formality and is characterized mostly by its naturalism. Its beds meander over a three-acre area from the East Portico of the Education Center to a curved trellis walk, and down a gentle slope toward water. In a growing season that extends well into fall, flowers of many colors and intensities cover the tops of thickly massed foliage.

This garden reflects the tastes of the late Bruce Krasberg, a board member of the Society and devoted rosarian. Mr. Krasberg himself had a substantial rose garden in the front of his home in Winnetka, and it was a constant wonder to passersby. But his interest in gardening propelled him in other directions as well. He was chairman of the Chicago World Flower Show in the period when the event was sponsored by the Horticultural Society. Under his direction in the 1970's, many garden clubs in the area participated with their most extravagant displays ever, built purely for the enjoyment of the public. He was president of the Men's Garden Clubs of America. And late in his life, Mr. Krasberg worked closely with rose society members in shepherding the development of the Rose Garden which would be named for him.

It was through Mr. Krasberg's own dedication that many local rosarians continue to work in maintaining this garden, and searching continually for the "perfect rose." Today, the Rose Garden has 100 taxa and 5,000 individual plants. They range from the vibrantly orange 'Tropicana' and the ivory white 'Garden Party,' which have proven to be hardy and reliable in this climate, to 'Rubrifolia,' which is as much enjoyed for its rich purplish foliage as its flower.

To achieve the best results, soil condition, pruning, watering and many other details are assiduously observed by those who care for the roses. But interest in this garden extends beyond the strict confines of the genus *Rosa*. It is planted with additions such as pagoda dogwood (*Cornus alternifolia*) and Red Splendor crabapple (*Malus* 'Red Splendor'), which flower early and also provide a setting of varied foliage. The result is a fully painted picture in which roses are the principal study.

Though the Rose Garden appears informal, its design has many carefully considered features. Among them is the Rose Petal Fountain, shaped like a finely opened flower. Placed near the far end of the garden, its waters draw visitors outward even on hot summer days. Also effective is the general arrangement of roses by color. The deepest-hued flowers are close to the front, the brightest farthest back, the result being that the eye can absorb the entire range from the East Portico viewpoint.

There's a seeming endlessness to the pleasures of the Rose Garden. Constantly, successively, strollers walk into fields of fragrance, often emanating from an identifiable source, sometimes not. 'Fragrant Cloud' is known for its heady, persistent scent. 'Double Delight' becomes particularly familiar for its spicy smell and unmistakable red and white pattern. Behind the trellis, a narrow path of polyanthus, shrub and other roses form a kind of netherworld, thick with color and fragrance.

No wonder, we might conclude, that roses have inspired literature of all kinds, from the ardent soliloquies of Shakespeare to pert rejoinders by Dorothy Parker. In classic illustrations of *Alice in Wonderland,* the card family played croquet beneath masses of floribunda. And more prosaically, rosarians often recount the botanical stories of many newer hybrids. The first budwood of the 'Peace Rose', for example, was rushed to the U.S. from France at the outset of World War II to avoid falling into German hands. By the war's end, it was ready for commercial production and much praise. Its pale yellow, pink-edged petals are almost suede-like in texture. 'Peace' provides even laymen with a glimpse into a kind of beauty that can be almost self-conscious in its intensity.

A wholly different world from the one that rosarians inhabit is found in the Farwell Demonstration Garden. Its long, winding path includes small cultivated habitats for herbs, perennials, ericaceous plants, water-loving plants, and many other forms. Its mission is to demonstrate how the best plants for the Chicago area can be effectively used in many different garden settings.

This garden is an appropriate tribute to the late Edith Foster Farwell, a well-known gardener, and with her husband Albert Farwell, an important benefactor of the Botanic Garden. She managed the Horticultural Society's Garden Center in Chicago after World War II. She wrote several books and other publications on gardening, and was gifted with clear insight into mankind's relationship to the earth.

Mrs. Farwell was regarded as Chicago's foremost expert on herbs, their history and uses. Aptly, the Herb Garden is a place where visitors can linger for long, restorative moments. Designed by Janet Meakin Poor, the Herb Garden winds through three separate "rooms," divided by living walls of pleached cockspur hawthorn (*Crataegus crusgalli* var. *inermis*) and Selkirk crab (*Malus* 'Selkirk'). Within these intimate spaces, a formal section is lined with boxwood and thyme, and centered with a traditional knot garden. Like similar designs at the Farwell's Lake Forest estate, the "knot" is a formation of small, close-growing hedges, planted to curve and intersect, and appearing as a loosely woven tapestry. The strands—lavender-cotton (*Santolina virens*), grey lavender-cotton (*Santolina chamaecyparissus*) and germander (*Teucrium chamaedrys*)—create an illusion of depth, intrigue the eye, and prepare the mind for other business still to come.

Throughout this garden, multifarious species invite us to reach down and stir fresh scents that penetrate the memory, and which some would say go deeper still. Herbs "change and alter my spirits and make strange effects in me," wrote a 16th-Century essayist quoted by Mrs. Farwell

Dedicated in 1988, the Dwarf Conifer Garden was funded by the Woman's Board. Since 1951, the Woman's Board has worked actively behind the scenes in support of the Horticultural Society. It maintained Society offices in the period before the Botanic Garden was built. The Board later donated a Fragrance Garden at the Chicago Lighthouse for the Blind. More recently it played an important role in developing the Garden's production greenhouses. With the dedication of the Dwarf Conifer Garden, the Woman's Board was recognized for nearly 40 years of enduring service.

in her book, *My Garden Gate is on the Latch*, "which makes me approve the common saying that the invention of incense and perfumes in churches…had a special regard to rejoice, to comfort, to quicken, to rouse and to purify our senses." Herbs, we know, were among the earliest plants to engage serious horticulturists. Today they are still popular, and still have the capacity to mystify.

Steps from the formal garden is an informal culinary planting, with a wattle fence made of bent willow branches. Shakespeare's medium of remembrance, rosemary (*Rosmarinus officinalis*), is prominent, with erect stalks and unmistakable scent. Seven different basils (*Ocimum* spp.) are here, each with subtly different profiles of lemon and licorice. More for the eye than the nose, a bed of intensely bright nasturtiums (*Tropaeolum majus*), with oval leaves that seem to float above their stems, complete this most civilized of feasts.

As our walk continues, we encounter arrays of perennials, chosen for this garden primarily because they flourish easily in our area. The path meanders through the "cool-color" beds, featuring salvia, iris, delphiniums and shrub roses, along with others that are profuse and harmonious through much of the summer season. More formal is a tall screen of arborvitae (*Thuja occidentalis* 'Techny'), backdrop to the traditional perennial garden, with plants as natural-looking as New York aster (*Aster novi-belgii*), others as fragile as Mt. Fuji phlox (*Phlox carolina* 'Mt. Fuji').

Farther on in the Farwell Garden water-loving plants have a home beside a small stream. The "fiddleheads" of cinnamon ferns (*Osmunda cinnamomea*) share space here with other narrow-leafed species, such as delicate 'Red Cloud' spiderwort (*Tradescantia virginiana* 'Red Cloud') and yellow flag (*Iris pseudacorus*), among others. Nearby, burnt-orange daylilies (*Hemerocallis* 'Brave World') and broad, handsome leaves of hosta (*Hosta longissima*) enjoy cool shade under a single elm and lindens that line this area. Amidst tufts of high grass we also find a stand of scouring rush (*Equisetum hyemale*), hollow shoots containing silica which pioneers used to wash their plates in streams.

Long before our own day, and our new-found respect for native plants, Mrs. Farwell's own mission was to provide a practical model for home gardeners. In spirit, this demonstration garden is like her own, "filled with so many of the humble, lovable old plants…which never look really happy in company with modern showy plants." While Garden curators also emphasize new, modern varieties that are practical for Chicago, this area reflects Mrs. Farwell's tastes, perhaps ahead of her time, which were not regal or grand, but a place for understated, simple pleasure.

Lilies enchant many garden lovers and it is not difficult to understand why. They are colorful and fragrant. They are often tall enough to stand handsomely with other plants. And they are long-lived, even permanent, if their bulbs are kept in well-drained soil, roots undisturbed, and a dozen other details well attended to. It is not an easy flower, say gardeners. Perhaps that is why their success is so rewarding.

In the Bulb Garden, *Lilium* 'Early Bird' comes up among the first, and rises to three feet before lifting its head with a beautiful brown-flecked orange flower. Then it threatens to fall over and tempts the doting gardener to pin it to stakes. Later lilies are more gregarious still. Sometime in June, regal lilies (*Lilium regale*) grow to a height of five feet. Purple on the rim of their flower trumpets and white on the throat, they are a comely companion to the purple smoke bush (*Cotinus coggygria*) which is nearby. And other flower combinations continue. The apricot 'Dawn Star' lily peaks over the top of fountain grass (*Pennisetum alopecuroides*), which itself forms a green backdrop for *Hemerocallis* 'So Lovely,' a greenish-yellow daylily.

Daylilies themselves are very popular, but they appeal to another side of the gardener's personality. They are a rugged plant with plenty of foliage, and for this reason they make good borders. Hemerocallis multiplies freely, resists weeds, and is permanent in most circumstances; the genus is not, apparently, preferred by insects. Along with hardiness, daylilies are also cooperative. Numerous cultivars have been developed, suitable for different zones, for specific height, and in colors from pale yellow to fiery crimson. Most curious, of course, is the flower. Among many that bloom on a stem over a period of several weeks, each one lasts for only a single day.

Paths lined by more lilies lead to water, where the boardwalk of the Kresge Aquatic Garden provides a setting for several plants, including the noble but aggressive lotus, and a selection of water lilies that are hardy in this climate. The magnolia water lily (*Nymphaea tuberosa*) is a native of Illinois and somewhat modest. Its counterpoint, the sweet-scented water lily (*N. odorata*), forms quickly-spreading clusters of foliage. And when the sun sets over the lake, they begin to close perceptibly. This quiet activity adds a touch of calm to an area that is otherwise filled with colorful, sometimes even foppish, behavior of garden lilies, which we gladly pass once again on our way home.

In all the Botanic Garden, the Regenstein Fruit and Vegetable Garden has the most utilitarian function. Nevertheless, it charms and attracts visitors for repeated strolls through kitchen gardens, a grape arbor and an industrious, small orchard. Other sections of the garden are ethereal, but here we see signs of intensive labor, which is truly part of the appeal. Beds are strictly organized. Details of planting and maintenance are taught. Volunteers at the plant information center are on hand to answer specific questions about soils, weeding, and the best varieties of fruits and vegetables for our area. There is even a demonstration kitchen where chefs from the Chicago area come to ply their trade for the education of the public.

Amidst all the business at hand, an undeniable romance pervades the Fruit and Vegetable Garden. It is designed in dimensions typical of a family residence. And while its scale might seem extravagant for a single

Plants are like people in several ways. They both need water, food, light and warmth.

From letters written by grade-school participants in the Children's Vegetable Garden

family, it points clearly to the fact that gardening as we know it probably began in a place not too different from this. In medieval Europe, according to a gardener's reading of history, families broke loose from feudal lords and built farmsteads where they lived a more independent life. Gardens were distinct from farms, according to landscape historian J. B. Jackson. "The garden, no matter what its size, called for incessant, detailed diversified work—a series of small chores, many of them requiring skill and judgment," Jackson writes in his book, *The Necessity For Ruins*. Given freedom from collective farms, people could experiment and learn to grow increasing numbers of vegetables.

It is obvious that life took on new pleasures with the development of asparagus, brussels sprouts and tomatoes, as they were dispersed widely and developed. Successful gardeners later cultivated fruit-bearing trees and gardens extended into orchards. Eventually, the prestige attached to growing abundant varieties led to the practice of building grand Renaissance pleasure gardens. Historians like Jackson see this, and the whole practice of horticulture, as a direct descendant of modest efforts to grow food for the kitchen.

But the Regenstein Garden's mission is not truly historical, rather practical. The best new cultivars of broccoli, cauliflower, sweet corn and even artichokes are planted and labeled. Grapes that are promising for our area also are being grown. And while many different apples are produced, the manner in which they are cultivated is sometimes as interesting as the fruit itself. *Espaliered* trees are grown flat against a brick wall. Near the grape arbor, a row of *cordons* are trained along a series of parallel wires. Both techniques are designed to maximize yield in a minimum of space. Beyond the arbor, dwarfed apple trees—with cultivars like 'Idared,' 'Red Haralson' and 'Redchief'—constitute a miniature orchard. It is a lovely demonstration of what is practical in smaller, more urban, environments where fruit trees are seldom considered.

Today, as in the distant past, gardens like this one benefit from undeniable public interest and scrutiny. Homegrown tomatoes are regarded as a substantial luxury. Freshly picked strawberries are reason enough for a weekend family outing. Elsewhere in the Botanic Garden, we might drift into wispy, imaginative worlds. But after a visit to the Fruit and Vegetable Garden, we return home wondering how we can possibly grow more interesting lettuce.

A great many impulses motivate horticulturists at the Botanic Garden, but underlying most of them is an interest in the relationship between people and plants. This is evident, perhaps more than anyplace else, in the Learning Garden for the Disabled. The area is not showy in the manner of other sections of the Garden. Yet its outcome is among the most satisfying. It demonstrates that plants provide rewards in the same measure that they are lovingly cultivated. This garden's lesson is that horticulture is therapy for persons with physical and emotional disabilities. Gardening relieves anxiety, lowers blood pressure, and provides many other benefits of physical activity.

The Learning Garden was the result of the Founders Fund Award of the Garden Club of America, and of the donations of several individuals. Its development was inspired and guided by the Kenilworth Garden Club, whose members understood that the first imperative of this, or perhaps any garden is that it meet practical considerations. So its paths are paved, and planters elevated, for easy access by people in wheelchairs. Plant types are carefully chosen. 'Better Bush' tomatoes are used here, essentially because they are short and reachable in raised beds. Heliotrope (*Heliotropum arborescens*) is popular for its rich, perfumy scent. And annuals—impatiens, marigolds, petunias and geraniums—are abundant in this garden, partly because the physical labor they require is therapeutic.

The Learning Garden is unique in many ways, but it is also like good gardens everywhere in that it communicates lessons about nature, and has the capacity to reach souls. There is something of that spirit also in the Smith Fountain, a large, explosive spray of water set out in the Garden's largest lagoon.

It is the most prominent fountain of many on the grounds, and even from a distance it appears three-dimensional. Like a garden itself, the Smith Fountain maintains a sense of drama—its structure is partially beneath the surface, but manifests itself splendidly in ephemeral arcs.

From various angles on a bright summer day, the Smith Fountain often casts a rainbow, one that is stunning for its size and proximity. This rainbow might be visible only from the Fruit and Vegetable island, or from the walk leading to the Heritage Garden. But it shines brightly, and it has the capacity, as surely as trees and flowers, to communicate an unmistakable message. A rainbow creates a special bond between a person and a place. And this, ultimately, is also the role of gardens.

Autumn

Sometime in August, a humid afternoon turns cold and rainy, and a distinct chill lasts a full day or even more. From that moment, we begin our personal relationship with fall. Instinct makes subtle adjustments. We watch for outward signs. True summer may persist, but well before the inevitable fall foliage, we are sensitized to flocks of birds, longer shadows, branches heavy with fruit. We prepare for fall carefully, hoping to relish its sensuous notes, trying to ignore its full message.

Fall is the emotional season. It is not sudden; it comes only in stages. But it resolutely replaces the torpor of the summer. We take in cold, astringent air which leaves us fresh and exhilarated. The evenings grow longer. Later on, color insinuates itself, then spreads. Where we once saw lush green walls, we notice random layers of color. The world becomes larger and it opens new moods.

We might have ended the summer as mere observers of nature. But in fall, we become participants. As temperature and color begin their changes, anticipation races. We luxuriate in ever lovelier tapestries, and dread their coming extinction. We hope, sometimes actively, to reconcile ourselves to autumn's retreat. Ideally, we prepare to go complacently into the grey existence of winter.

At the Botanic Garden, the first notes of autumn are camouflaged in an area where a rich palette of natural color has held forth since midsummer. It is the Garden's prairie developments, fifteen acres that appear properly untouched, but where naturalists are resurrecting plant communities that existed in the Midwest before settlers arrived. As they also do in the Turnbull Woods savanna, they have undertaken to manage the prairie with fire.

The Chicago area lies within a salient of the vast prairie land that used to stretch, for thousands of years, across Iowa, Kansas and Nebraska. But its deep, fertile topsoils have been depleted ever since 19th-Century "sod busters" put plow to earth. Prairie, which once covered two-thirds of this state, now accounts for less than one-tenth of one percent. Tall grasses that were ubiquitous are now considered "ornamental." And once-plentiful wildflowers are threatened with extinction.

As part of the prairie project, the Garden has replanted native species, grasses such as big bluestem (*Andropogon gerardii*), Indian grass (*Sorghastrum nutans*) and others that previously flourished in this setting. To clear aggressive plants that could push out prairie natives, naturalists now conduct spring fires that once took place naturally, assisted by the turpentine-like resins in some plants. These clear dead grass and early growing weeds, making way for deeply rooted wildflowers—white wild indigo (*Baptisia leucantha*), prairie dock (*Silphium terebinthinaceum*) and compass plant (*Silphium laciniatum*) among others—that are beginning to reestablish themselves here.

The prairie takes on an iridescent glow by September. Big bluestem is now bright russet in color. And "pioneer plants," so-called because they move opportunistically into areas disturbed by buffalos or wagons, have reached a colorful peak. Among them, asters (*Aster* spp.) grow in large violet bunches. White boneset (*Eupatorium perfoliatum*)—an American native considered medicinal by settlers—covers portions of the prairie with white, cotton-like clouds. Patches of bright yellow goldenrod (*Solidago* spp.) also attach themselves to the soft contours of this fine country quilt. Only later do their colors dissolve in a veil of morning mist and frost.

As the season moves on, the overall intentions of fall become clear. Some years, of course, the color is subdued unto drab. Other years it provides all the calico of postcards and imagination. But fall theatrics cannot be predicted. Rainfall, it is suggested, influences color, but so do soil, temperature, length of days and other conditions. They change every year. While the outcome may be subject to scientific explanation, the script is never known until the performance unfolds.

Even in subdued autumns, the Botanic Garden is taut with potential for drama. A walk through the demonstration gardens, for example, starts impassively enough, with ground cover of stoical English ivy (*Hedera helix*), a leafy evergreen, and cockspur hawthorns (*Crataegus crusgalli*) still verdant and summer-like. But amidst affectations of permanence, there are other signs. Almost innocently, autumn crocuses (*Colchicum autumnale*) poke through the ivy, seducing us with new color, encouraging us to go on.

In the Bulb Garden, heaps of autumn clematis (*Clematis maximowicziana*) project sweet perfume in a place where most fragrance is long gone. Annabelle hydrangea (*Hydrangea arborescens* 'Annabelle') persists now with a subtle silvery tone, later deepening to brown. Ozawa flowering onion (*Allium thunbergii* 'Ozawa') stands upright in a sort of lonesome perfection. Each plays a separate role in the articulate fall opera.

The human hand needs to be given due credit. In the Landscape Demonstration Gardens, a sedum hybrid called 'Autumn Joy' has been cultivated to explode with tiny crimson flowers just now. Apple serviceberry (*Amelanchier xgrandiflora*), placed amidst more subdued shrubs, shows rusty red in leaves that turn early and hold on until late. Perhaps most memorable, winged euonymus (*Euonymus alata*) is bright fuchsia, almost spot-lit in intensity, and appears otherworldly against a backdrop of rich evergreens.

The Searle Courtyard features a fountain of 49 subterranean jets of water, providing coolness and light within the brick walls of the Education Center. It is one of many generous contributions made by the G.D. Searle Family to the Horticultural Society. The Garden's prairie development and its horticultural therapy program are funded in part by contributions from the Searles. The family has also provided a major endowment for horticultural research at the Botanic Garden.

The herb gardens have been largely cleared and put to rest for the season by early October, but some perennials are still in the ground, winding themselves down to dormancy. Western sage (*Artemisia ludoviciana*) hugs the ground this time of year. It is a nearly luminescent silvery grey, and its small leaves now fill the hand with an agreeable, savory scent. Nearby, thyme is fading, but even in cool air it is an aromatic signature of a traditional herb garden.

Fall casts its influence inscrutably. The Rose Garden, now with the last of its 'Peace' roses and other hardy varieties, distinguishes itself with masses of conspicuously crimson foliage. Behind the arbor, floribunda and polyanthus shrubs provide fall color in their leaves, while their flowers still resist any suggestion of cooler weather. And nearby, the Japanese garden is characteristically serene, with the exception of isolated cotoneasters and other bushes blazing like ruby-colored jewels on their large green background.

When we walk along the winding path of the James Brown IV Waterfall Garden, we are enveloped by a fall setting as striking as any place in the Botanic Garden. Water appears to flow, as if by plausible magic, out of the top of the earth. This would have pleased the late James Brown, executive director of the Chicago Community Trust and board member of the Horticultural Society. He was known for his interest and love of fountains. The Waterfall's granite boulders, brought here from Wisconsin, form pooled terraces that punctuate the soft flora of the slope. The sound of rushing water is persistent but intimate. Perhaps the most curious effect of the Waterfall Garden is that it foreshortens perspective, making it look higher than its mere forty-five feet.

Autumn comes to the Waterfall dramatically, but also with its share of mixed signals. The cutleaf staghorn sumac (*Rhus typhina* 'Laciniata') is fiery by mid-September with its intense saffron fall color. But while some plants react quickly to cool evening temperatures, small flowers like the azure monkshood (*Aconitum carmichaelii*), with a cluster of elfin "hoods" on each stem, stay happy in the fragile morning warmth. Weeks later, the sun recedes further and flowers go ragged. But for consolation, a black maple (*Acer saccharum* ssp. *nigrum*) shows a yellow so intense that it seems to serve as a light source all its own. And among many other colorful specimens, a particular poiret barberry (*Berberis poirettii*) maintains its rich green on the outside while interior branches are transformed with streaks of purple, orange, yellow and many intermediate shades. What mysteries lie in this species? How long will this fancily woven textile last?

Inevitably, we reach the Waterfall's summit. The water source remains hidden beneath ground cover, but from this highest point in the Botanic Garden we look over nearby maples and hickories and ashes. Beyond is Turnbull Woods, whose colored treetops form distinct layers, a dozen of them, amplifying both altitude and distance. It is quiet at the summit, even when people are about. It is an opportunity to suspend time, imprint this memory of evanescent tapestries. It is also a moment to contemplate the significance of nature's compulsion to spend its last sensate moments in such an interesting and lovely blaze.

Winter

The monochromes of the season draw long panoramic lines across the land. The low sun casts long shadows which dramatize gentle folds in the terrain. The Botanic Garden is never more graceful than it is in winter. It provokes the imagination. The mind can make easy leaps to picture the Garden once again in flower, but in winter the scenery is reduced to certain essentials.

A walk outdoors in winter reinforces many important messages of the Botanic Garden. One is that this is a place of many separate, but contiguous, vantage points. Now, as always, the Garden features a succession of views—over lakes, to shores, from hillocks and out to streams and orchards—all harmonized as if painted on a long scroll to be revealed only portions at a time.

The visitor's eye in winter grows sensitive to subdued but distinct details. The forms of the Dwarf Conifer Garden stand out prominently, and as curiously as ever, when partially covered with snow. In the Japanese Garden, cotoneasters expose their compact, angular stem patterns, born of years of careful pruning. In the Farwell Garden, the pendulous bare branches of a weeping beech (*Fagus sylvatica* 'Pendula') drape down and brush the snow-covered ground. Everywhere, oaks and maples show their black tracery against the steel-grey sky.

In closer detail, a discernible winter's palette emerges. Bright red fruits of Winterking hawthorn (*Crataegus viridis* 'Winterking') can persist until New Year's, by which time they are picked clean by birds. Apple serviceberries (*Amelanchier ×grandiflora*) have silvery bark which can shimmer on a clear winter day. Bright copper leaves hang on to shingle oaks (*Quercus imbricaria*), and the red stems of redosier dogwood (*Cornus sericea*) are handsome against wide evergreen curtains.

Interest in the winter garden extends beyond things botanical. An absorbing calm pervades the ground covered with snow. Deer tracks show us that they live more leisurely, perhaps more social lives when the grounds are largely deserted of people. Red fox are known residents, and they leave lighter, more solitary tracks.

Nearly silent outside, the Garden contains busy indoor activity in the Nancy Race Educational Greenhouses. Three glasshouse clusters are devoted to demonstrating often amazing details in the lives of plants. In one, we witness how plants adapt in specific ways to climate and other conditions. The sun-loving ficus tree (*Ficus benjamina*), for example, scrapes against the glass ceiling, while the saddle-leaved philodendron (*Philodendron selloum*) grows large and heavy in relative shade. The greenhouses are warm and suited mostly to tropical and subtropical species. But their needs are varied, and each plant is labeled with optimal temperature, moisture level, soil profile, and the amount of daily sunlight that the species prefers.

Interesting adaptations are illustrated by "carnivorous" plants, such as pitcher plants (*Sarracenia* spp.), which have slender tubes into which insects fall and drown, and Venus fly trap (*Dionaea muscipula*). A fine display of topiary also resides here, showing the various textures of exotic herbaceous plants, and the whimsical nature of gardeners who use them to sculpt penguins and camels.

Another set of greenhouses is designed to point to the provident nature of plants, from the refreshing color of James Walker bougainvillea (*Bougainvillea* × *buttiana* 'James Walker') to the broad-leafed ti plant (*Cordyline terminalis*) which is used in warm climates both for sugar molasses and the thatched roofs of dwellings.

The sculpture of William H. Turner and his son David is known for authenticity in anatomy, expression and behavior. "Flying Geese," dedicated in 1989 to the memory of Marion Miller Bent, captures an important element of activity at the Botanic Garden. Many types of wildlife, including Canada geese, have made the Garden their home throughout the year.

The third greenhouse complex, devoted to adaptations in desert environments, houses a large collection of cacti. The thick stems of these succulents store water, and sharp spines protect many of them from thirsty predators. That is what they have in common, but we also can observe that strategies for survival in this climate can vary a great deal. The fine, bleached hairs of old-man cactus (*Cephalocereus senilis*) shade this species from sun and protect it from the wind. Among the loveliest plants of the desert is *Agave colorata*, with its cone-like shape appearing solid as porcelain, and with tips colored of the deepest indigo.

Winter also provides time to investigate practical gardening techniques that can be used later on. In the Zimmerman Lecture Series, diverse ideas related to horticulture and landscape architecture are presented by speakers from around the world. Honoring the late Board Member Elizabeth Zimmerman, these lectures explore design and ecological issues that can influence the private gardens of Chicago and the surrounding area.

Aspects of winter make it an appropriate time for art. Colors outside are muted, and the light seems far away. But in winter, the Garden's strengths are more vivid than ever. Boxwood hedges are especially linear when they hold a layer of snow. The bluish-green needles of Scots pine show beautifully against its cinnamon-brown bark, colors that are enriched by the low-lying sun. Snow blows and drifts in patterns reminiscent of clouds in the sky, begging for an added measure of definition in a painting or photograph.

It is also a season to witness outdoor sculpture and architecture. "Composition in Stainless Steel," by Gidon Graetz, gleams in the snow-covered Rose Garden. "Great Blue Heron," by Gregory Glasson, stands out strongly in a perennial border now otherwise bereft. From a distance, the Education Center, designed by architect Edward Larrabee Barnes, is more striking than ever, hugging the ground with strong horizontal lines, and piercing the sky with graceful tower and pyramids. The Theodore C. Butz Memorial Carillon, now silent, stands handsomely against the sky on Evergreen Island.

It is an ascetic time. But winter's insularity is often penetrated by the striking images created by commonplace events—such as the russet glow around the shadows of a snow-covered landscape. Winter shows an underlying structure, frozen but not forbidding. It is as relaxing and as dream-laden as a long, well-earned rest.

The Future

Change is the essence of gardening, and the Botanic Garden keeps changing in many encouraging ways. Green backdrops grow larger, seasonal color is evermore more heartening, and the Garden's palette of plants increases with each passing year.

To build an evermore delightful garden, designers are at work developing new settings. Horticulturists apply their skills to maintain an unparalleled variety of plants. And a commitment to research promises to add to the Garden's, and to the region's, inventory of hardy species. The outcome of these efforts is a continuously magnificent Garden that consistently penetrates our spirit.

The ornamental function of the Botanic Garden—an exquisite success since its groundbreaking twenty-five years ago—is entering new phases. An English Walled Garden has been planned by designer John Brookes to evoke pleasures that harken back to medieval Europe, and settings in which shrubs, vines and flowers provide architectural links between closely set buildings. Walled gardens are characterized by warmth and varied charms.

The design of this "private paradise," enclosed by brick walls and hedges, will feature an approach through a small wooden gate, beyond which is planned a Courtyard Garden, donated by Marianne and Bruce Thorne. The courtyard is to be paved with random-sized square stones, and filled with familiar plants—serviceberry, azalea, spirea and others. In dimension and in character, the courtyard provides a kind of home gardener's idyll.

The Walled Garden will have a complex of other sections, each distinct but all composing a graceful whole. The Formal Daisy Garden is to be abundant, even overflowing with flora, underlain by a backbone of strong, definite lines. Beds are to be planted principally with members of the sunflower family, all with radiating florets, and in a strong, bright palette.

From the Daisy Garden, visitors will descend gentle steps through a balustrade to the Sunken Garden. Given in honor of Henrietta Louis and her children, this section will be centered with an octagonal pool. Perennials—*Geranium, Iris, Veronica* and many others—will grow all around. The Sunken Garden is to be partially enclosed by an old English wall, and in time, its crevices will fill in with *Sedum, Thymus,* hens and chicks (*Sempervivum*), lady's mantle (*Alchemilla*) and other leafy plants. These and other touches suggest permanence, similar in some ways to Great Dixter, Christopher Lloyd's famous garden in Kent, England.

A Cottage Garden is to be the most naturalistic space in the Walled Garden, and most evocative of an outpost in the English countryside. A casual feel characterizes cottage gardens. They are not manicured, but seem to thrive on their lack of strict cultivation. "A cottage garden is essentially a profusion of old fashioned flowers—both perennial and of favourite shrubs and shrub roses," writes Brookes. "Its colours are soft and gentle, and its vines and roses reach up into the arms of gnarled old apple trees."

A Pergola Garden, given by Mary and John P. Bent, is planned for the farthest end of the Walled Garden. This section will feature a wisteria-shaded arbor, in which one can sit and look over a fountain splashing in a small pool. Lutyens benches, with camelbacks, will be set along gravel pathways. This is essentially a modest, enchanted area, with borders that will overflow with the blues and purples of *Campanula, Echinops, Delphinium* and *Salvia.*

The final portion of the Walled Garden will lie along its northern extremity, a narrow footpath filled with layers of color and waves of fragrance. This section has been donated by Patricia and Kenneth Bro, and is dedicated to Patricia's mother, Elizabeth Price Welch. It will feature dozens of different species, each playing its role in a garden that provides year-round interest. Old-fashioned lilacs will lace the garden in spring. By summer, woodbine honeysuckle vine will blossom extravagantly on the inside wall. Nearby butterfly bush (*Buddleia*) will attract colorful, animated butterflies. Low-growing shrubs—such as viburnum and cotoneaster—will be accompanied by plume poppies (*Macleaya cordata*), growing seven feet high, among many other distinctive perennials. Even in winter, hydrangea will show full flowerheads, dried and cream-colored, long after the growing season has ended.

A flight of steps is to lead to a grassy bank, and large shade trees will eventually create an area with the effect of 18th Century English parkland. Along an exterior length of the wall, a fifteen-foot wide perennial

The Botanic Garden has grown faster than any of us in our wildest dreams would have imagined when we began. I remember that people said the Garden would never be finished, which is, in a sense, true. On the other hand, we have built something, in only 25 years, that is very beautiful. So many people have taken an interest in it. It answers such an important need. That is why the Garden has grown as quickly as it has.

Peter H. Merlin, Chairman, Board of Directors, 1972-1979

bed, given by the Woman's Board, will provide space for perennials that might be too large for other gardens. These include obedient plant (*Physostegia*), rhubarb (*Rheum*) and black-eyed Susan (*Rudbeckia*), along with an assortment of shrubs.

For twenty-five years, the Botanic Garden has planned and built dramatic settings to touch the imagination of visitors. While continuing to achieve aesthetic marvels, the Garden of the next decade will more forcefully influence the environment of our entire region. In recent years, the Garden has undertaken the painstaking, but ultimately rewarding, work of plant evaluation and development. The splendor of gardens depends no less on these scientific efforts than on the large canvas of landscape design. By developing new plants that are hardy in our region, the Garden adds to its own aesthetic variety. More broadly, this work addresses the needs of threatened native species which by themselves cannot compete against the reduction of natural habitat. Horticulturists can reverse unfortunate trends, expand our region's palette of plants, and ultimately produce a visible, permanent effect on cities, towns and gardens throughout our area.

New genetic material comes to the Botanic Garden from many different sources. Garden horticulturists, for example, make expeditions to the wild to seek pure specimens of plants that once flourished in our climate zone. By cultivating these plants, curators can find and develop new strains which are tolerant of ecological stress. This role, as a Noah's Ark for plants, will lead to untold benefits as years pass and the environment changes still further.

Efforts to create promising new species also depend upon alliances between the Botanic Garden and other groups. Chicagoland Grows Inc. has joined together the Garden, The Morton Arboretum, and the Ornamental Growers of Northern Illinois to introduce new plants for general use in our region. Chicago Lustre viburnum was among the first successful plants created through this venture. Meanwhile, several national plant societies—devoted to ivy, boxwood, holly and others—are assisting the Garden to conduct long-term evaluations of certain species and cultivars for our climate zone.

As the Garden matures and its role as a major cultural institution expands, it also increases as a resource to interpret the botanical world. The June Price Reedy Horticultural Library holds a collection of 10,000 volumes, including rare books and historical hand-colored illustrations. The library serves the research of horticulturists, historians and others whose work involves plants and gardens. Art has long served as an inter-

Nancy Race was one of the most dedicated, devoted people that the Garden has ever had. As a Board Member, she could be found anywhere she was needed, in meetings or by herself working with plants. She was also concerned with presenting horticulture so visitors could understand it, so they could see beautiful plants and learn to grow them at home. The Educational Greenhouses are a tribute to Nancy's interest in interpreting the world of plants for people.

Betty Bergstrom, Vice President of Development, discussing the late Nancy Race, Chairman, Board of Directors, 1986-1987

preter of nature, and to this end the Museum of Floral Arts, given in memory of Edward Carson Waller, houses a collection of painting, sculpture, textiles and other art forms that use plants and landscape as their inspiration. In still other ways, music is a spiritual companion to gardens, and the Theodore C. Butz Memorial Carillon produces lovely shaded harmonies in concerts that range from classical music to children's folk songs.

As it begins its second century, the Chicago Horticultural Society has resolutely expanded its vision beyond the 300 spacious acres of the Botanic Garden itself. In its mission to stimulate and develop an interest in gardening among all people, the Garden has established a presence throughout the Chicago area, in many branches of community service, and especially in urban neighborhoods. These efforts involve outreach to public schools, in therapeutic settings, and in the building of vegetable gardens on vacant lots in the city. Wherever space exists and interest can be cultivated, the Botanic Garden's role is to encourage gardening of all kinds.

Such work is eminently practical, but it is motivated by a deep philosophical commitment to creating a greener and more vital environment throughout our region. As an educational and inspirational resource, the Garden continually expands its influence with its gentle but urgent message: That regeneration and beautification rest on a fragile ground.

As we encourage gardeners, we create more than green backdrops for fine color. Plants are nature's most visible and responsive offspring. As we witness their fine performance, we simultaneously foster greater respect, even awe, for the forces of nature that make it possible. Nature teaches its profound lessons in many ways. At the Botanic Garden, and through its many outreach programs, we learn that gardens do more than simply enhance the quality of our lives. They are an integral part of the human spirit.

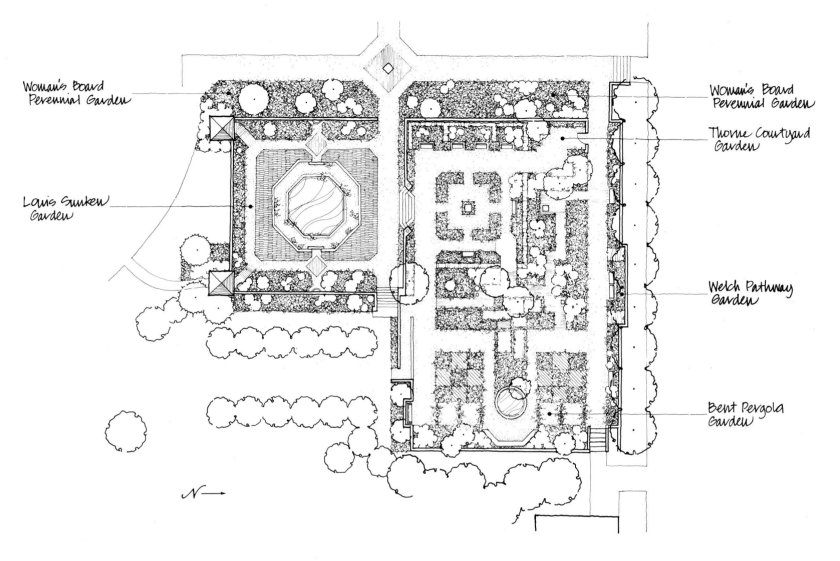

Woman's Board
Perennial Garden

Louis Sunken
Garden

Woman's Board
Perennial Garden

Thorne Courtyard
Garden

Welch Pathway
Garden

Bent Pergola
Garden

N →

*Plan of the English Walled Garden,
designed by John Brookes.
A watercolor (left) of a detail
of the English Walled Garden:
an overview of the Sunken Garden,
dedicated to Henrietta Louis
and her children.*

Chicago Horticultural Society History:

1890-1990

History of the Chicago Horticultural Society

and Chicago Botanic Garden

Through the Years

1837
Chicago adopts for its corporate seal the motto *Urbs in Horto*—"City in a Garden."

1853
John Wright and Dr. John Kennicott, editors of the *Prairie Farmer,* urge that Chicago acquire 300 acres of land on the outskirts of the city for parks and a garden. The Chicago Botanic Garden, on a 300-acre tract, would be created by an act of the legislature 110 years later.

1867
The informally organized Chicago Horticultural Society holds its first flower show in Crosby's Music Hall.

1890
The Horticultural Society of Chicago is incorporated by the State of Illinois on October 1. George Schneider, editor and activist, serves as first President. Other significant figures are John Beveridge, former Illinois governor; Jonathan Periam, *Prairie Farmer* editor; and J.C. Vaughan, seedsman.

1893
At the World's Columbian Exposition, Society members participate in Horticulture Hall, a 187-foot dome of steel-frame construction. George Schneider raises $135,000 to help save the fair from financial ruin in the Panic of 1893. J.C. Vaughan's prize gladioli launch his international reputation.

1907
The Society's flower shows, held each November in the Chicago Coliseum and other sites, are recognized as "the largest and most successful flower shows on this continent," by a contemporary reporter. Mrs. John J. Glessner, whose home is now a museum in Chicago's Prairie Avenue Historic District, serves as chairman of the Lecture Committee.

1908
Horticultural Society forms relationship with Art Institute of Chicago, due in part to Charles Hutchinson, a founding trustee of the museum, and President of the Horticultural Society. Flower shows and gardening lectures would be regular events at the Art Institute through 1918.

1917
The Cook County Forest Preserve District purchases Turnbull Woods. Other parcels, which today comprise the Chicago Botanic Garden, would be purchased between 1921 and 1950.

1933
Century of Progress features five acres of gardens. Although the Horticultural Society is currently inactive, those involved include several members who would revive the Society a decade later.

1937
The Society's state charter is allowed to lapse.

1943
Spurred by the Victory Garden movement of World War II, Park District officials and others seek to revive the Society. Charter is reinstated under the name of the Chicago Horticultural Society and Garden Institute.

1945
Society holds first Spring Garden Meeting, which would be for many years an annual event to recruit new members.

The first *Garden Talks* (later *Garden Talk)* is issued in April. A photo shows a flag flying over a vegetable garden with the caption: "Oh! Long may it wave, o'er gardeners loyal and gardeners brave."

1951
The Woman's Board is founded, and authorized to assist in building membership rolls, initiate new programs, sponsor and conduct fund-raising projects, and advance the goal of the Society to open a permanent headquarters and garden center.

1952
Luncheon is given November 13 to celebrate the 62nd anniversary of the Society's founding. Many descendants of original members attend.

1953
Garden Talks is reinstituted as the publication of the Society. President Elmer Claar publicly urges Chicagoans to garden.

1954
The Society adopts Chicago Horticultural Society as its official name.

The Society distributes 10,000 hyacinth bulbs to Cook County school children, providing many with their first gardening experience.

The Woman's Board announces plans for the Fragrance Garden to be built at the Chicago Lighthouse For the Blind.

1955

At the Society's annual meeting, President Milton Carleton presents 13 hybridizers with the Society's Certificate of Merit. Those honored are: Elmer Claar, peonies, iris and daylilies; David F. Hall, iris and daylilies; Hubert A. Fischer, iris and daylilies; Richard Goodman, iris; Glenn Pierce, miniature gladioli; Carl Klehm, peonies; G.E. McKana, columbines; Brother Charles Reckamp, iris; E.L. Hodson, iris and daylilies; Nathan H. Rudolph, iris; Orville Fay, iris and daylilies; Arthur Murawska, peonies; Paul D. Voth, daylilies.

1956

Fragrance Garden at Chicago Lighthouse For the Blind—the largest herb garden in the Midwest—is dedicated by the Woman's Board.

1957

Gardening program for handicapped children begins at the Christopher School in Chicago, with Society assistance. Alice W. Burlingame, a national leader in horticultural therapy, comes to Chicago to consult in this project.

1959

The Chicago World Flower and Garden Show opens at the International Amphitheatre with Society participation that would last through 1979.

1961

The Society endorses idea of a conservatory and "great horticultural center" for Chicago. Dr. Carleton argues for the need saying, "Chicago is half a century behind the rest of the United States in the development of horticultural facilities."

1962

After discussions with Mayor Richard J. Daley, the Society begins to seek land for a garden of its own. President William A.P. Pullman identifies Glencoe site and devises a plan to lease this property from the Cook County Forest Preserve District.

1963

Attendance at the Chicago World Flower and Garden Show is listed at 353,000.

The Grant Park Rose Garden is planted near Buckingham Fountain with more than 8,000 plants donated by leading growers. A plaque is installed by the Society to commemorate its participation in the project.

The "Botanic Garden bill," under the sponsorship of Rep. Frances Dawson of Evanston, passes state legislature, and enables the leasing of Forest Preserve land in Glencoe.

1964

Pullman reports that the Society has raised $1 million, which is a legal condition for creation of the Botanic Garden.

1965

The Cook County Board of Supervisors approves an ordinance for the Society to use the 300 acres of Forest Preserve land. It authorizes a tax levy to maintain the Garden.

Ground is broken for the Chicago Botanic Garden on September 25.

1967

Dr. Francis de Vos becomes the first Director of the Botanic Garden. The first trees are planted along Edens Expressway.

1968

Dr. George W. Beadle, Nobel Prize-winning geneticist and President of the University of Chicago, is elected President of the Chicago Horticultural Society.

1969

Water comes to the Botanic Garden— 190 million gallons of it. "The bumps in the topography become islands, and the graceful curves of the land defined," reports *Garden Talk.* Ground is broken for the first permanent buildings.

1970

Construction is begun for the Home Landscape Center near the Dundee Road entrance. Six gardens are planted nearby.

1971

The Junior League of Evanston consults with Dr. de Vos about volunteer projects at the Botanic Garden. Initially, they agree to act as tour guides.

A demonstration vegetable garden is planted, and markers are installed along a nature trail in Turnbull Woods.

Chicago World Flower and Garden Show returns to the rebuilt McCormick Place.

Dr. Louis B. Martin elected President of the Society. He comes to Chicago from the Brooklyn Botanic Garden where he was director.

1972

The Chicago Botanic Garden celebrates opening with formal dedication.

1973

Plans are announced for the Education Center, to be designed by Edward Larabee Barnes. The Building Committee accompanies this announcement with the remark, "The individual seeking knowledge and real-life experience with living plants will be able to do so with almost total lack of interference and congestion, in an atmosphere of quiet but vigorous activity." The Building Committee includes James Brown IV, Mrs. C. Phillip Miller, Lewis J. West, and Peter H. Merlin.

1974

Garden Club of America presents its $5,000 Founder's Fund Award to the Society for installation of a horticultural therapy garden. It will become the first garden in the nation completely designed for use by the handicapped.

1976

The Botanic Garden's Education Center is dedicated. The building features a 200-seat auditorium, exhibition hall, meeting room, museum, library, classrooms, gift shop, restaurant, and educational greenhouses. Two courtyards flank the exhibition hall: the Frances

Runnels Courtyard, and the Searle Courtyard containing the Searle Fountain.

Learning Garden for the Disabled, demonstrating how people with physical disabilities can enjoy gardening, is dedicated.

Dr. de Vos announces he will leave on January 1, 1977, to become director of the University of Minnesota Landscape Arboretum and a professor of horticulture.

1977
Dr. Roy Mecklenburg, associate professor of horticulture at Michigan State University, is named President of the Chicago Horticultural Society and Director of Chicago Botanic Garden.

1979
Society membership reaches 3,564. More than 280 volunteers provide 14,000 hours of service.

1981
Home Landscape Demonstration Gardens are dedicated, including five specially designed gardens: Edith and Albert Farwell Herb Gardens, Perennial Gardens, Ericaceous Garden, Rock Garden and Viburnum Walk.

The Smith Fountain, in memory of Mr. and Mrs. Harold Cornelius Smith, is dedicated.

1982
Sansho-En *(Garden of Three Islands)*, a "promenade" style Japanese Garden covering 17 acres, is dedicated.

The Pullman Plant Evaluation Garden, to study new plants for introduction in the Chicago area, is dedicated.

1983
The Kresge Aquatic Garden and the Edna Kanaley Graham Bulb Garden are dedicated as new parts of the Home Landscape Demonstration Gardens.

1984
The Gertrude B. Nielsen Heritage Garden, with a sculpture of Carolus Linnaeus, is dedicated. Based on the design of an early botanic garden in Padua, Italy, its plantings are grouped by family and place of origin, with labels to help visitors understand taxonomic classification, and Linnaeus's role in establishing it.

The Ellen Thorne Smith Naturalistic Garden is dedicated as part of the Home Landscape Demonstration Gardens.

1985
The Regenstein Fruit and Vegetable Garden is dedicated on its own 3.8 acre island.

The Bruce Krasberg Rose Garden and Rose Petal Fountain are dedicated.

The Mesic Prairie is dedicated as a native-Illinois, tall-grass prairie. Marsh Island, the wet-prairie area, will be dedicated in 1987.

Dr. Roy L. Taylor becomes Director of the Garden and President of the Society. He was Director of the Botanical Garden at the University of British Columbia in Vancouver.

1986
The Theodore C. Butz Memorial Carillon is dedicated on Evergreen Island. Forty-eight bronze bells weighing from 24 pounds to 2½ tons were cast in the Netherlands for inclusion in the 60-foot tower.

Site for English Walled Garden is dedicated by H.R.H. Princess Margaret.

The Botanic Garden receives museum accreditation status from the American Association of Museums.

1987
The William T. Bacon Sensory Garden for the Visually Impaired is dedicated. Mr. Bacon was one of the founders of The Hadley School For the Blind.

Greenhouses in Education Center are dedicated as the Nancy Race Educational Greenhouses.

1988
James Brown IV Waterfall Garden is dedicated. The hillside garden of winding paths features a waterfall that drops 45 feet across a series of granite terraces.

The Dwarf Conifer Garden, a gift from the Woman's Board, is dedicated. This hillside garden displays genetically dwarfed specimens of common evergreens.

A Perennial Test Garden is established as a research plot to determine the best herbaceous flowers for the Chicago area.

1989
First Lady Barbara Bush visits the Garden on April 26.

Groundbreaking is conducted for English Walled Garden.

1990
The 100th anniversary of the formation of the Chicago Horticultural Society, and the 25th anniversary of the Chicago Botanic Garden are marked in a ceremony on September 8.

No history of the Chicago Horticultural Society would be complete without acknowledging the scholarship of Suzanne Carter Meldman, who spent three years researching and writing the booklet, *The City and the Garden: The Chicago Horticultural Society at 90,* published in 1980.

Awards of the Society

Charles L. Hutchinson (1856-1924) was the founder and president of the Art Institute of Chicago, a banker, the president of the Chicago Board of Trade, and a board member of many civic organizations, including the Chicago Horticultural Society.

On a trip to Europe in 1894, Hutchinson commissioned Swedish sculptor Henning Ryden, who earlier had studied at the Art Institute, to create a medal for the Horticultural Society. It was cast in Paris in that year, but records indicate that only one recipient was honored with it in Hutchinson's lifetime: Edwin L. Kanst in 1911.

When Paul L. Battey became President of the Society in 1951, he appointed Jesse L. Strauss to convene an Awards Committee to reinstitute the medal. Service to horticulture in the Chicago area was to be honored, and recipients were to be chosen every year.

In 1982, the Awards Committee decided that "the Hutchinson Medal should reflect the growing national and international reputation of the Society and Garden." National stature in horticulture henceforth would be among criteria for the award.

In the same year that the Hutchinson Medal was broadened in scope, the Society also established the Chicago Horticultural Society Medal to recognize "outstanding service of basic and enduring benefit to the Chicago Horticultural Society."

In 1983, the Linnaeus Award was established to recognize lifetime contributions of individuals involved in developing new plants for American horticulture.

Hutchinson Medal Winners

1911 Edwin A. Kanst, long-time Chicago Park District employee and son of one of the earliest board members of the Society.

1951 Edith Foster Farwell, known as one of the foremost advocates of organic gardening in the Midwest. She maintained an extensive herb garden. She served on the Society board, and was active in the Garden Club of America and the Lake Forest Garden Club. She was a founding member and later president of the Woman's Board. In 1973, she would receive the Achievement Medal from the Garden Club of America.

1952 Jean Morton Cudahy, daughter of Joy Morton, who was founder of The Morton Arboretum. She was chairman of the Arboretum from 1934 to 1953, and was central in programs benefiting crippled children in Chicago.

1953 Oakley Morgan, horticulturist for Commonwealth Edison Co. He was a member of the Society's board, a leader in Chicago's Victory Garden program during World War II, and one of the founders of the Men's Garden Clubs of America.

1955 David Francis Hall, a hybridizer of iris and daylilies. He was also honored in his lifetime with the Foster Memorial Plaque of England for outstanding work in hybridizing, and awards from the Men's Garden Club of Chicago, and American Iris Society.

1956 Fred Heuchling, longtime Chicago Park District information director who headed the Victory Garden campaign during World War II, and who helped revive the Society in 1943. He was the voluntary executive secretary of the Society from 1950 until his retirement in 1960. He founded the Society's library with donations

from members, inaugurated *Garden Talks* as the newsletter of the Society, arranged garden tours and a television series, directed adult education courses at high schools, and developed a school children's project.

1957 Nels J. Johnson, tree care expert whose Evanston tree company was established in 1930. His efforts to protect homeowners from fraud led to legislation requiring licensing of tree experts.

1958 John Nash Ott Jr., who pioneered time lapse photography of plants in his Lake Bluff greenhouse. He became a member of the Board of Directors in 1961.

1959 R. Milton Carleton, Ph.D., research director of Vaughan's Seed Co. in Downers Grove, a nationally recognized horticulturist, author and lecturer. He received this award for his service to the Society as President for three years, his research, and his authorship of articles and books on gardening.

1960 Garden Club of America, Central Western Zone, which contributed to the success of the Chicago World Flower and Garden Show.

1963 Hubert A. Fischer, an outstanding amateur gardener known for his breeding work with hemerocallis, iris, daffodils, peonies and Oriental poppies. He was elected to the board in 1954.

1967 Clarence E. Godshalk, an employee at The Morton Arboretum when construction began in 1921. He eventually served as its director for 32 years. He was one of the founders of the American Association of Botanic Gardens and Arboreta.

Charles (Cap) G. Sauers, General Superintendent of the Cook County Forest Preserve District for 35 years and national authority on wildlife preservation. He was instrumental in convincing the Cook County Board of the need for a botanic garden.

1968 William A.P. Pullman, President of the Society from 1960 to 1968. He was the guiding force behind the creation of the Chicago Botanic Garden.

1969 Virginia Carlson, director of the Society's Garden Therapy Program since its inception in 1957. She was "The Flower Lady" to physically and mentally handicapped pupils at many Chicago schools.

1970 John Lundgren, chief horticulturist of the Chicago Park District. "Look around you in Chicago and wherever your eye lights upon living plant material, the chances are perhaps 10 to 1 he has had a hand in bringing it into being," his award citation read.

1972 May Thielgaard Watts, naturalist of The Morton Arboretum from 1942 to 1961. She started education programs at the Arboretum and was an internationally known teacher. She authored *Reading the Landscape* and *Reading the Landscape of Europe.*

1973 Eric Oldberg, M.D., longtime member of the Board of Directors, and later its Chairman. His work was instrumental in gaining the support of governmental bodies, enabling the Society to get the land and financial resources to build the Garden.

1975 Art Kozelka, garden editor of the *Chicago Tribune.* "He spreads the gospel of good horticulture throughout mid-America by means of his perceptive, enthusiastic articles," wrote Mrs. Margaret McClure, chairman of the Awards Committee.

1976 Richard J. Daley, Mayor of Chicago, for his energetic support of the Chicago World Flower and Garden Show, the Society, the Botanic Garden, and the general beautification of Chicago.

1977 Franz Lipp, noted landscape architect who designed the plantings at Cantigny Gardens and Museums, and the Runnels and Searle Courtyards of the Education Center at the Chicago Botanic Garden.

Anthony Tyznik, landscape architect of The Morton Arboretum. He was honored, among other reasons, for excellence in design of displays at the Chicago World Flower and Garden Show.

1978 James Brown IV, executive director of the Chicago Community Trust and a Society director for 19 years. He was instrumental in raising the first $1 million for the garden in 1964. He promoted gardening in Chicago's inner-city schools.

Bruce Krasberg, who joined the Society in 1946 and served on the Board of Directors for 34 years. He was chairman of the Chicago World Flower and Garden Show for nine years. For his contributions to the Society, the Krasberg Rose Garden was named in his honor. He served as president of the Men's Garden Clubs of America.

1979 Edward Larrabee Barnes, who designed the Education Center. The award-winning architect designed many museums around the nation, including a restoration project at the New York Botanical Garden.

John O. Simonds, landscape architect who developed the Master Plan for the Botanic Garden. The project involved shaping a whole new landscape of hills, streams, lakes and islands. Simonds began garden construction in 1966 and won several awards for his work.

1980 Arthur Janura, General Superintendent of the Cook County Forest Preserve District. "His understanding of the ecological processes has enabled him to develop comprehensive programs to replant forests, restore prairies and decrease the pollution of streams and lakes," read the citation which accompanied his award.

Peter Merlin, the Society's legal counsel during negotiations with the Forest Preserve District, and Chairman of the Board from 1972 to 1979. He "inspired the board to

begin a capital campaign to raise the $8.5 million for the Education Center and to bring that drive to a successful conclusion," read his citation.

1981 Rose Vasumpaur, a founder of the Woman's Board, whose garden was the scene for many plant sales, with proceeds being donated to the Society. A garden consultant with a trove of horticultural knowledge, she shared her love of gardens with thousands of people in the Chicago area.

Garden Clubs of Illinois, honored for 50 years of promoting indoor and outdoor gardening.

1982 Donald R. Egolf, Ph.D., breeder of woody plants at the National Arboretum in Washington, D.C. He developed 30 new shrub cultivars, 14 of which were planted in the Garden's Virburnum Walk.

1983 Herbert C. Swim, rose breeder, who developed more than 100 new roses, 25 of which were selected for All-American designation, more than any other breeder.

1984 Robert F. Carlson, Ph.D., and Joseph S. Vandemark, Ph.D., who planned and developed the Regenstein Fruit and Vegetable Garden. Dr. Vandemark, professor emeritus at the University of Illinois, was one of the Midwest's leading authorities on vegetable production. Among his extensive writings is *Vegetable Gardens for Illinois.* Dr. Carlson was professor emeritus in the department of horticulture at Michigan State University, and the nation's leading authority on dwarf fruit trees.

1985 William T. Stearn, Ph.D., former president of the Linnean Society (1979-1982) and retired Senior Principal Scientific Officer, Department of Botany, the British Museum. Known as the world's leading authority on Linnaeus, he advised the Botanic Garden on the design of the Heritage Garden.

1986 Peter H. Raven, Ph.D., director of the Missouri Botanical Garden, St. Louis. Under his leadership, his garden has developed a tropical botany research project that supports rainforest conservation efforts in Central and South American countries.

1987 John L. Creech, Ph.D., former director of the National Arboretum in Washington, D.C. He is a renowned plant collector and geneticist, and has been instrumental in the introduction of Asian plants in America.

1988 Mildred E. Mathias, Ph.D., professor emeritus of botany, University of California at Los Angeles. She is a national leader in plant research and conservation activities.

1989 Vernon T. Heywood, plant systematist, author, and leader in developing a worldwide program of plant conservation through development of the Botanical Garden Conservation Secretariat, Kew, England.

The Chicago Horticultural Society Medal

1981 Francis de Vos, Ph.D., the first Director of the Chicago Botanic Garden.

1982 William A.P. Pullman, honored for decades of contributions to the Society.
   Elizabeth T. Zimmerman, honored for technical knowledge in horticulture and long-time service to the Society and Woman's Board.

1983 Nancy Zimmerman Race, Vice Chairman of the Board, and later to become Chairman of the Board in 1986.

1984 George W. Dunne, Chairman of the Cook County Board of Commissioners, for his long-time support of plants and greenspace in and around Chicago.

1985 Ralph A. Bard Jr., Chairman of the Board from 1979 to 1987, oversaw the construction of the majority of demonstration and display gardens.
   Janet Meakin Poor, landscape designer who designed the Farwell Herb Gardens, and who would become Chairman of the Board in 1987.

1986 Ruth Hodges, manager of the Garden Shop, a fund-raising component of the Woman's Board.
   Ralph Synnestvedt Jr., president of Synnestvedt Nursery Inc. He was a board member from 1979 to 1989, and was chairman of the Botanic Garden Committee, which reviews garden design.

1987 Mary McDonald, chairman of the Botanic Garden Committee of the Cook County Board of Commissioners and Forest Preserve District.

1988 Bruce Krasberg, honored posthumously for his contributions to the Society, as a board member and the chairman of the Flower and Garden Show, and for the cultivation of roses.

The Linnaeus Award

1983 Brother Charles Reckamp, of Techny Mission, Ill., honored for his breeding work on iris and daylilies. He introduced more than 150 varieties of daylilies, and more than 40 varieties of his iris. He also developed Techny arborvitae.

1984 Andrew Tures, of Matt Tures Sons Nursery of Huntley, Ill., honored for his contributions to the woody ornamental industry in Illinois.

1985 M. Leider and Sons, Inc., for continuing dedication to excellence in foliage plant production and distribution.

1986 Edmund Mezitt, president of Weston Nursery, Hopkinton, Mass., for his development of hardy rhododendrons.

1987 William Flemer III, president of Princeton Nurseries, Princeton, N.J., a leader in the development and introduction of woody ornamentals.

1988 The producers of the Public Broadcasting System program "The Victory Garden," a long-running, nationally televised series.

1989 Richard A. Jaynes, Ph.D., president of Broken Arrow Nursery, Hamden, Conn., honored for his selection, breeding and introduction of new varieties of Kalmia.

Flower Shows

Gardens were an early touchstone for Chicagoans, and local organizations were active in competitions and shows almost from the city's founding. In 1849, a group by the name of Chicago Horticultural Society published rules for its garden competition in the *Prairie Farmer* newspaper. By 1867, this group organized a flower show at Crosby's Music Hall. At that event, the cut flowers of one E.B. McCragg were singled out for mention. He was a local florist whose greenhouses would survive the Chicago Fire in 1871.

In 1888, the Chicago Florists Club instituted an annual flower show. This was a time of much activity in local horticulture. In 1890, the Chicago Horticultural Society was incorporated, in part to plan horticultural displays at the World's Columbian Exposition. The Society began its annual Autumn Exhibition in 1892, which was held that year and for several years thereafter. Phillip D. Armour, one of the Society's directors, offered $125 for the winning chrysanthemums at the inaugural event.

By 1908, the Society and its events became associated in the public mind with the Art Institute. A succession of shows were held there, and lectures delivered. The largest shows at the museum were remembered as sumptuous affairs. Hundreds of chrysanthemums, carnations and other plants were entered, and huge plants were often transported by boxcar from Eastern estates for display in Chicago.

Between the World Wars, the Society was largely inactive. But in 1959 it once again was involved in important flower shows, with the first annual Chicago World Flower and Garden Show, held that year at the International Amphitheater. Frank Dubinsky was managing director of the show, and would remain so for 14 years. Harold O. Klopp served as the principal landscape architect for displays during this period.

In 1961, the show moved to the newly constructed McCormick Place, where it occupied 222,000 square feet of floor space. By this time, the Horticultural Society was the event's full sponsor. It was attended by hundreds of thousands of Chicagoans each spring for most of the decade.

The flower and garden show was a huge undertaking for the Society. Each year, the Woman's Board organized a fund-raising preview to open the show. And Horti-Court, an amateur plant competition that would continue for many years at the Botanic Garden, was a mainstay of the show.

In 1967, ten weeks before the show's opening, fire ravaged McCormick Place, and momentarily left the fate of the Chicago Flower and Garden Show unclear. A Herculean effort on the part of Society Director Robert Wintz and others transferred the entire event to the Amphitheater, where it remained for two years.

Moving back to the rebuilt McCormick Place in 1971, the show became the largest of its kind in the nation. Chicago rosarian and Society board member Bruce Krasberg was chairman of the show for the next nine years, and it attracted 200,000 annually during this time.

After 1979, the Society withdrew from this show, determining that it should concentrate on year-round displays and demonstration gardens at the Chicago Botanic Garden. In this way, the Society would maintain its traditional role as host of the city's, even the nation's, most lavish and important flower shows.

Administration of Society

Chairmen of the Board

1969-1972 Eric Oldberg, M.D.
1972-1979 Peter H. Merlin
1979-1986 Ralph A. Bard Jr.
1986-1987 Nancy Zimmerman Race
1987-   Janet Meakin Poor

Presidents of the Chicago Horticultural Society

1890-1891 George Schneider
1891-1905 William H. Chadwick
1905-1908 Edward G. Uihlein
1908-1910 William E. Kelley
1910-1912 Charles Hutchinson
1913   Willis N. Rudd
1943-1944 Carl Kropp (acting)
1945-1949 C. Eugene Pfister
1949-1951 Paul Battey
1951-1953 Elmer Claar
1954-1955 F.A. Cushing Smith
1956-1960 R. Milton Carleton, Ph.D.
1960-1968 William A.P. Pullman

*A change in the Society's policy made the Presidency
of the Society and Directorship of the Botanic Garden
a single paid position, beginning in 1969.*

1968-1971 George W. Beadle, Ph.D.
1971-1977 Louis B. Martin, Ph.D.
1977-1985 Roy A. Mecklenburg, Ph.D.
1985-   Roy L. Taylor, Ph.D.

Chicago Horticultural Society

Board of Directors 1965 to 1990

Howard D. Adams	1986-		James Brown IV*	1965-1984	
Michael Allik	1982-1987		A.C. Buehler Jr.	1974-	
Mrs. James W. Alsdorf	1975-		J. Melfort Campbell	1980-	
Mrs. Robert W. Anderson	1989-	*ex officio*	R. Milton Carleton, Ph.D.*	1955-1969	
Andrew A. Arentz	1979-1981		Mrs. Robert Adams Carr	1967-1969	
Mrs. Pamela K. Armour	1978-		Kent Chandler Jr.	1981-	
William T. Bacon Jr.	1985-		Irving W. Colburn	1960-1967	
G. Carl Ball	1978-1980		Mrs. Ann D. Cook	1972-1974	
Ralph A. Bard Jr.	1978-		William H. Cooley Jr.	1988-	*ex officio*
George W. Beadle, Ph.D.*	1966-1975 *Life Director*		Donald C. Cottrell Jr.	1977-1979	
Gordon Bent	1981-		Mrs. John S. Dean III	1987-	
John P. Bent	1986-1989		James G. Dern*	1966-1976	
Edwin A. Bergman*	1972-1978		Mrs. James G. Dern	1975-1978	
Mrs. Betty H. Bergstrom	1976-	*ex officio*	Leonard D. Dunlap	1978	
Harold G. Bernthal	1978-1979		George W. Dunne	1969-	*ex officio*
Edward Bodde	1977-1980		Howard A. Emig*	1955-1972	
John A. Bross Jr.	1970-1981		Robert S. Engelman	1985-1987	
Mrs. Gardner Brown	1983-		Mrs. Ralph Falk II	1974-1985	

List of Plates

Pages 2 and 3
Merrill magnolia
Magnolia ×loebneri 'Merrill'
Island west of Education Center

Page 4
Creme de la Creme lily
Lilium 'Creme de la Creme'
Edna Kanaley Graham
   Bulb Garden

Page 8
Wonderland Iceland poppy
Papaver nudicaule 'Wonderland'
Gertrude B. Nielsen
   Heritage Garden

Page 10
Snow Bunting crocus
Crocus chrysanthus 'Snow Bunting'
Edna Kanaley Graham
   Bulb Garden

Page 12
Beverly crabapple
Malus 'Beverly'
Farwell Demonstration Garden

Page 14
Small-cupped narcissus
Narcissus sp.

Page 15
Red maple
Acer rubrum
Unsurpassable narcissus
Narcissus 'Unsurpassable'
Across water from Edna Kanaley
   Graham Bulb Garden

Page 16
Star magnolia
Magnolia stellata
Daffodils and leather bulb tulip
Narcissus ssp. and *Tulipa praestans*
Edna Kanaley Graham
   Bulb Garden

Page 17
Jupiter guinea-hen flower
Fritillaria meleagris 'Jupiter'
Tête-à-tête narcissus
Narcissus 'Tête-à-tête'
Edna Kanaley Graham
   Bulb Garden

Pages 18 and 19
Weeping willow
Salix alba var. *tristis*
Merrill magnolia
Magnolia ×loebneri 'Merrill'
Education Center

Page 20
European white birch
Betula pendula
South of Nancy Race
   Educational Greenhouses

Page 22
Juneberry (foreground)
Amelanchier canadensis
Apple Serviceberry
Amelanchier ×grandiflora
Turnbull Woods

Page 24
Large flowered trillium
Trillium grandiflorum
Turnbull Woods

Page 25
White and pink flowering
   dogwood
Cornus florida and
Cornus florida 'Rubra'
Turnbull Woods

Page 27
River birch
Betula nigra
Along north road

Page 53
Snow Queen columbine
Aquilegia ×hybrida 'Snow Queen'
Farwell Demonstration Garden

Page 54
Globeflower
Trollius europaeus 'Superbus'
Columbine meadowrue
Thalictrum aquilegifolium
Connecticut Yankees delphinium
Delphinium 'Connecticut Yankees'
Gertrude B. Nielsen
 Heritage Garden

Page 55
Dazzler tickseed
Coreopsis tinctoria 'Dazzler'
Lavender cotton
Santolina chamaecyparissus
Tattletale coral bells
Heuchera sanguinea 'Tattletale'
Farwell Demonstration Garden

Page 56
Wild columbine
Aquilegia canadensis
Bleeding heart
Dicentra spectabilis
William T. Bacon Sensory Garden

Page 58
Virginia rose
Rosa virginiana
Sedge
Carex sp.
Gertrude B. Nielsen
 Heritage Garden

Page 59
Peace rose
Rosa 'Peace'
Bruce Krasberg Rose Garden

Page 60
Medallion rose
Rosa 'Medallion'
Bruce Krasberg Rose Garden

Page 61
America Rose
Rosa 'America'
Bruce Krasberg Rose Garden

Pages 62 and 63
Gene Boerner rose
Rosa 'Gene Boerner'
Bruce Krasberg Rose Garden

Page 63
Duet rose
Rosa 'Duet'
Bruce Krasberg Rose Garden

Page 64
Whirly Bird nasturtium
Tropaeolum majus 'Whirly Bird'
Informal Herb Garden
Farwell Demonstration Garden

Page 65
Formal Herb Garden
Farwell Demonstration Garden

Page 67
Shortleaf white pine
Pinus strobus 'Brevifolia'
Nanho Purple butterfly bush
Buddleia davidii 'Nanho Purple'
Hudson spruce
Picea glauca 'Hudsonii'
Weihenstephaner Gold stonecrop
Sedum floriferum
 'Weihenstephaner Gold'
Blue Carpet singleseed juniper
Juniperus squamata 'Blue Carpet'
Dwarf Conifer Garden

Page 68
Mauve catnip
Nepeta mussinii
Dreamglo rose
Rosa 'Dreamglo'
Bruce Krasberg Rose Garden

Pages 68 and 69
Nearly Wild Rose
Rosa 'Nearly Wild'
Russian Sage
Perovskia atriplicifolia
Carolus Linnaeus by
 Robert Berks
Gertrude B. Nielsen
 Heritage Garden

Page 70
Daylily
Hemerocallis 'Ruffled Ballet'
Gertrude B. Nielsen
 Heritage Garden

Page 72
Northbrook Star daylily
Hemerocallis 'Northbrook Star'
Farwell Demonstration Garden

Page 73
Purple coneflower
Echinacea purpurea
Prairie Song daylily
Hemerocallis 'Prairie Song'
Farwell Demonstration Garden

Page 74
Regal lily
Lilium regale
Edna Kanaley Graham
   Bulb Garden

Page 75
Regal lily
Lilium regale
Edna Kanaley Graham
   Bulb Garden

Page 76
Regenstein Fruit and
   Vegetable Garden

Page 77
Purple Spires loosestrife
Lythrum salicaria 'Purple Spires'
William T. Bacon Sensory Garden

Page 78
Children's Vegetable Garden

Pages 80 and 81
Regenstein Fruit and
   Vegetable Garden

Page 81
Beta grape
Vitis 'Beta'
Regenstein Fruit and
   Vegetable Garden

Page 82
French marigold
Tagetes patula 'Janie Yellow'
Swiss chard
Beta vulgaris 'Vulcan'
Better Bush tomato
Lycopersicon lycopersicum
   'Better Bush'
Learning Garden for the Disabled

Page 84
Skokie River in late summer

Page 85
Carolina poplar
Populus ×canadensis 'Eugenei'
Along Edens Expressway

Pages 86 and 87
Smith Fountain in north lagoon

Page 87
Sawtooth sunflower
Helianthus grosseserratus
Prairie area

Page 88
Hill's oak
Quercus ellipsoidalis
Turnbull Woods

Page 90
Common ironweed
Vernonia fasciculata
New England aster
Aster novae-angliae
Switch grass
Panicum virgatum
Old witch grass
Panicum capillare
Prairie area

Page 91
Sawtooth sunflower
Helianthus grosseserratus
Big bluestem
Andropogon gerardii
Tall goldenrod
Solidago altissima
Common milkweed
Asclepias syriacus
Prairie area

Page 92
Sawtooth sunflower
Helianthus grosseserratus
Tall goldenrod
Solidago altissima
Hairy aster
Aster pilosus
New England aster
Aster novae-angliae
Prairie area

Page 93
Late boneset
Eupatorium serotinum
Tall boneset
Eupatorium altissimum
New England aster
Aster novae-angliae
Tall goldenrod
Solidago altissima
Prairie area

Page 94
Morning mist, early October
Prairie area

Colophon

Inspiration for *A Garden For All Seasons* came in 1988, two years before the Chicago Horticultural Society's Centennial Anniversary. The objective of this book was to record one hundred years of history at the Society, and also convey the radiance of the Chicago Botanic Garden.

Because of their intense interest in conservation, gardens and local history, members of the Harold Byron Smith Family agreed to support this project. Christopher Byron Smith, David Byron Smith, Harold Byron Smith, Jr., and Stephen Byron Smith influenced the book in many ways. It has been dedicated to their father, Harold Byron Smith, a longtime member of the Board of Directors.

Arthur Lazar was chosen to photograph the Garden, an assignment that required continuous contact with the Botanic Garden for a full year. His love of gardens is combined with an extraordinary feel for rich and varied color—his photographs truly speak for themselves.

Jay Pridmore wrote the accompanying essays. The text demonstrates an appreciation for the inscrutable forces of nature that lie beneath the surface of the Botanic Garden, and also includes lively insights into the Horticultural Society's history and influence on Chicago. Mr. Pridmore is a journalist who has written widely on topics related to cultural institutions.

William A. Seabright undertook overall responsibility for the production of *A Garden For All Seasons.* Mr. Seabright, an award-winning book designer, assembled many parts to produce a work of great impact and fine detail. His patient and sensitive counsel was valued by all those who worked with him.

Many other people were involved in *A Garden For All Seasons.* Among them, William Aldrich worked as archivist on the project, which will serve as a valuable historical resource for years to come. Much credit for this book's appearance goes to Nisha Printing, Ltd., Kyoto, Japan, and its representative, Toshio Ohsa. Nisha has produced books and catalogues for many of America's finest museums.

Richard DiPietro, president of The Typesmiths, Inc., of Chicago, provided much support in assuring a book of high quality in every detail. This required patience and generosity, in addition to a staff of extraordinary skill.

The insight and enthusiasm of directors and staff at the Chicago Horticultural Society and Botanic Garden were invaluable in the publication of this book. Janet Meakin Poor, Chairman of the Board, combined her knowledge of gardens with an appreciation for the book's graphic and textural details. Director Roy Taylor and Assistant Director Kris Jarantoski, more than anyone, were responsible for the scientific correctness of the book. The entire Botanic Garden staff, especially Horticulturist Galen Gates, and many volunteers were helpful in many ways to bring the book to completion.

Most of all *A Garden For All Seasons* owes its existence to Betty Bergstrom, Vice President, Development, who overcame all obstacles in realizing a book that matches the splendor of the Botanic Garden itself. Mrs. Bergstrom's loving, judicious eye was present at every step in the process. Anyone who appreciates the result owes her a debt of gratitude.